Contingency

*Selected, Collected Poems,
Volume Two
1989-2001*

James Howard Trott

*Oak and Yew Press
Philadelphia*

Contingency

Selected, Collected Poems, Volume Two
1989-2001

James Howard Trott

**Copyright 2015
James Howard Trott**

**Oak and Yew Press
Philadelphia, PA**

CONTENTS

	page
Contingency	1
Weaker Eyes	1
Another Compass	2
Aphid Feathers	2
The Blind Crooner	3
A Chipmunk Encountered	3
The City Screamed	4
God Rules With An Iron Rod	5
The Distillation	6
Enough For Today	7
Fishing Off Warren Island	8
Street People	8
The Fulfillment Of Desire	9
Piñata	9
Dust-Up	10
Cybernetics	10
Yesterday's Salt	11
Grains Of Snow	11
Threshold Pain	12
Heaven Is A Windy Place	12
Around The Block Or With A Pillow Over My Head	13
Herod's Welcome	14
I Don't Call It Anything	14
Others Lives	15
I Want To Be At Everybody's Picnic	15
'Spoiled Child	16
The Laser Beam	16
Babel (Victoria)	16
Lids And Lips	17
Simon The Blind Magician	18
Midnight Waking	20
Closed Eyes	20
Naked And Insane	21
The Hose Not Taken	22
Stare Decisis	23
No Spoils	23
A Squirrel In A Tree	24
I Pray I Will Know My Pisgah	24

Freddy	24
Called Out Of Egypt	25
The Old Man	26
Translator	26
Our Weary Heads	27
Helen Launched	27
The Poet As Alchemist (For Robert Duncan)	28
The Right Sort Of Bang	30
Second Best	31
No Runt In The Litter	31
Semi-Private Hell With Detached Bath	32
Derelict	32
Sing Me	33
Foxfire	33
Heaven Dropped The Baby	34
You Can Go Home Again	35
The Foolish Things To Confound The Wise	35
Squirrel Shadow	36
Woods Into Winter Night	36
Step Of Faith	37
Wheel Weights	37
Still Life	38
Useful Stuff	38
The Swift	38
Two Kings Wept	39
The Tank	40
Teaching Credentials	41
Two Day Storm During Harvest	41
Alpha And Omega	42
To Donkeys Everywhere	43
A Thin Tune	44
To All The Secret Celibates	45
Time In The Attic	45
Tears Of Sowing	46
The Heavenly City	46
Switchbacks	47
To A Child Learning To Dive	48
Spring Is Not As Warm	48
Undergoing Privation	49

Silence Sends Messages	49
The Waiting Room	50
Searching The Stones	50
Vehemence	50
Political Economics	51
Save Or Spend	51
The Wedding Rehearsal	52
Worship Dancers	52
Prophetic Utterance	53
Present Faith	53
Angels Of Promise And Doom	54
Portable Dungeon	55
The Executioner	55
Pharoah's Butler And Pharoah's Baker	55
Ark On The Plains	56
Arrest	56
Perpetual	57
Information Revolution	57
The Painted Trees	58
The Bachelor's Bowl	58
Owing To What	59
How Art The Fallen Mighty	59
Opening Others' Presents	60
Part For Whole	60
On This Wet Morning	61
Burglar's Fingerprints	62
On Reflecting on Saint Boniface	62
Chewing Diamonds	63
The Occasion Of A Poem	63
This Is A Desert Place And Now The Time Is Far Passed	64
Not Enough	65
The Cry Of The Deaf	65
No Judas	66
Degradation Looking Good	66
Missed Kiss	68
The Sensitive Fern	68
Memory Fades	69
Denying An Inferno Fuel	70
Living Large	71

Margaret	71
Spring Ferns	71
Like Raindrops	72
A Dramatic Production	72
Letter To Edward And Emily	73
Eavesdropping On Angels	74
Learning Curve	74
Are You The Man?	75
Leapfrog	76
Empty Handed Again	77
Faith Questions	77
It's Scary To Watch People Marry	78
For Richer Or For Poorer	78
Is God?	79
Not Spells But Prayers	79
The Independent Scribe	80
Nakedness Is Not Just Skin Deep	80
If Crime Is Natural	81
Grace Is Found In Low Places	81
The Harp Of God's Guts	82
Sliding Scale Of Significance	82
Hap Hazard	83
Graving Images	83
Guerillas Going In	84
Once Seven	85
The Glory Of The Laurel	85
Herod And Judas	86
God's Bare Body	86
The Two Organs Of Sex	88
For Heaven's Sake	89
High Gull	89
First Clues	90
Things Buried	90
Firefly Code	91
Honor Among Thieves	92
Fire Building	92
Images Of Christ	93
Fall Fish	93
Night's Lady	94

Faint Disapproval	95
It's Wrong To Die For The Dead	95
Exuberance And Enthusiasm	96
Jawbone Of An Ass	97
Empty Package	97
Explorer	98
Laocoon	99
Washing Wayward Feet	99
Eli Sat	100
Rules Of Precedence	100
Early Contender	102
Mowing The Neighbor's Lawn	102
Until I Am Distraught	103
Cost Accounting	103
Crossing The Red Sea	104
Offerings As Whiskey	105
Courts Poet	106
God Is Not Careful	106
Conspicuous Keys	107
Old Stump, New Tree	107
Comes Around	108
On A Novel With Missing Pages	111
Clay And Potter	112
Christ As Projection	113
The Opposite Of Incarnate	113
Paper Significance	114
Bushwhacking	115
Eliezer Fishing In Samaria	116
Breaking Weather	116
Use Us - Three Interpretations	117
A Billion Dollar Attitude	117
Explicit	118
Azalea Weather Indicators	118
Balanced Account	119
Predator	119
As Each Loves	119
The Wasting Of Our Powers	120
Alien Shores	121
Put It Out Of Its Misery	121

Abandoned	122
Rabbit Trails	122
Bribes And Threats	123
Your Tears Are Blurring My Vision	123
Right Index	124
Where Is God When It Hurts?	125
Faith's Antonyms	126
The Welder's Torch	126
A Saw Only Cuts When It Moves	127
Walking Toward My Father Walking Away From Me	127
Sin Bound	128
Unfinished Business	129
Every Man's Hour	129
Touch And Go	129
Staring At The Sun	131
Tobacco Smoke And Coffee	132
Tether Ball	132
Time To Be Glorified	133
The Thinker	133
There Is A Burglar In My House	134
Fruiting Due To Trauma	135
Sudden Frost	135
The Third Storm (For Nancy Long)	136
Stripped Body On A Cross	137
Time To Kill	137
The Splinter	138
Communion Images	139
One Of The World's Best Lovers	140
Obituary For Frances Whittington	140
The Right Way To Respond To A Gift	141
Light Of A Certain Kind	142
Least Leading	142
The Truly Self-Righteous	143
In Memory Of Ethel Vile	143
Underwhelmed	144
Vision From Our House	145
A Warm Front	145
Gerry's Departure	145
Higher Glyphics	146

Detritus And Treasures	146
Desperate Rose	147
We Doubt	147
What The Snow Did	148
Deliver Me Into The Deep	148
Locksmith : Keys Made	149
The Companion	150
Why We Ignore The Dying	150
Clean Hands	151
Black Walnuts	152
Between	153
Without Practice	153
I Am The Proprietor Of The Baseball Booth	154
Being Hugged Behind My Back	155
You Never Pick Trash In Your Own Neighborhood	155
Alpenglow	156

James Howard Trott

CONTINGENCY

Contingency's snarled my well-laid lines,
Laid many an hour, many a day,
Has mocked my marathon, made a joke,
A to-and-fro of fits and starts.
Though I know myself part of a kind of plan,
And sense deep down a solemn calling
Into noble deeds and magnificent tasks
For completion at lofty points of time,

Contingency claims me, rules my life:
Will allow me no inertia to build;
Denies my longings, ekes off efforts,
And erodes my earnest effects into silt.

What kind of God cares thus for me?
What kind would submit to contingency?

WEAKER EYES

As I grow older and my eyes weaker,
I am able to see the sunlight vary
Against the trees and clapboard walls
As the clouds shift over the sky.
This is new to me. I now see
In a way I never could
When my eyes were more agile,
Could more quickly compensate
For variations in the light.
I miss more as my eyes grow weaker,
But see what I see by as my sight fails.

Contingency, Poems 1989-2001

ANOTHER COMPASS

My attitude, my angle of repose,
Heaven knows, is not to rest at all,
But pivot and sweep across the dial
Of life and cosmos. East and west, rise and fall,
My little needle runs away from
Every cardinal point in epileptic imitation --
Of the clock's hands... ordained but ever moving --
No -- fluttering in frantic declination.

First I tend south, dive the dial to soothless self;
Swing away west, rest horizontal on phenomenal
    mankind's shelf;
Plunge back around east, lying backward, wishing death;
Shun always north like metronome set to runner's breath,

Though that heavenly magnet near the stellar pole
Without mercy, still demands my soul.

APHID FEATHERS

That miniscule pest of garden and pot
Also renowned for the friendship it's got
With the ant, who protects it for honeydew,
The aphid, has feathers like me and you.

It's digestion is abominable -- aphids can't
Digest the nectar which they pass to the ant,
Nor the waxy substances their bodies exude
Like little feathers without which they're nude.

Though tiny, a respectable aphid in feathers
Is quite striking, airy-plumed in still weathers;

But alas, when a wind blows with too much vigor,
The aphid is much reduced as a figure.

The feathers are records of successful feeding
(Perhaps to aphids indicate good breeding),
But like our diplomas, resumes and accounts,
In the storm aphid feathers don't weigh an ounce.

THE BLIND CROONER

We didn't want to be there,
On the New York subway
In perpetual musk of
Urine, sweat, and lonesome.

When we got on the train,
A blind man entered
With eyes of dusk
But a voice like an angel.

Winsome, gentle, through a microphone
He addressed us directly,
Blessed him who gives,
Coins clanked in his box

Something down here lives!

A CHIPMUNK ENCOUNTERED

I wandered lonely as a crowd
Among tree, bush and flower

Contingency, Poems 1989-2001

At the edge of a clearing
Where unconsciously nearing,
I surprised him in his bower.

A dapper-striped creature in a forked wand
Of blueberry out in the sun,
Lying, eyes hooded like one who dreams
Who muses over what is and what seems,
Enterprises barely begun.

I walked towards him subtly, silent, sly
At every step winding again and again,
My film and each time clicking the shutter
Until in my progress smooth as butter
I stood at his door like a friend.

The portrait I took at that bare remove
Is a study in miniature worry.
Having taken it, I had to relent,
And so, still quietly, on I went,
Leaving him thoughts wild and furry.

Such proximity never would have occurred
To a chipmunk better in wisdom seasoned.
All others seem to keep their distance
I make no claim to rodent omniscience
But the munk-chit must have reasoned:

"It might not see me, it will soon go past,"
Like other small minds, while yet they last.

THE CITY SCREAMED

I sat bolt upright. Roseann did, too.

James Howard Trott

"What was that noise!" "I don't know... no clue!"
So I leaped from bed and fumbled for glasses,
(Which took ages to find -- dimly time passes!)
Then I stood at the window and saw -- only
The leaves of our tree, the street dark and lonely,
The cars parked, the houses closed,
Both our seeing and wishes to our hearing opposed.
I went downstairs and out, in pajamas
So compelling that yell, conjuring such dramas
Of horror, of murder, of violence near us --
Close to home where terror is sheerest.
I looked in our yard and between the cars,
Went across the street and peered through bars
Of neighbors fences, seeking relief
Of fears of finding, then thought, 'the police'.
I asked her to call them, soon they came,
Heard the scream echo through my tale of the same;
Then searched the block front, and the streets around,
But at last went away, nothing been found.
We called a few neighbors, but conviction was growing
A deeper fear, a heart-sprung unknowing
That the call of agony, as of one badly dreaming
Was in fact the sound of the city screaming.

GOD RULES WITH AN IRON ROD

God rules with an iron rod
Held in invulnerable hand.
He rules the wind and the waves and me
None can argue with such as He,
Nor the iron rod in his hand.

Like the merciless blows of steely fate
(God rules) or fickle lightening or hate,

Contingency, Poems 1989-2001

None knows when he will strike them down
Or who will be driven into the ground
By the iron rod in his hand.

It seems useless to live as though reward
Awaited us -- rather a sword
To annihilate us like vermin or dust,
Swept from his floor, scoured off like rust
On the iron rod in his hand.

God! If there were but one way under
The rod unassailed, nor broken asunder,
Shattered like chaff, like windblown grass-stems,
Wasting their whispers, prayers, "ah-mens"
Upon the flailing rod.

But, oh, the tale they tell (not well)
Of the day God traded heaven for hell
And rather than handling whips or flails
Forged his rod into iron nails
And took them into his hands.

THE DISTILLATION

My lady has lost her lethargy,
My lord exhausted ambition.
What sort of retort their chamber,
So to refine their condition?
Some reification they have undergone
That their tempers are made so pure,
Driven away duress and dross --
He sleeps and she is sure.

James Howard Trott

ENOUGH FOR TODAY
(On the proper salary for ministry)

The supper came first in the world reversed
Where He blessed what was cursed from the start of time.
And divinity winked over things once distinct
'This is my flesh, which is broken through;
This is my blood, all of you drink,
It must last me 'til home
Where again I feast with you.'

But it was not the last, no He did not fast,
Not many hours passed before He drank more.
And with wine on his brow, asked his Father somehow
If this last cup might not pass from him.
'But you are the vintner,' he amended
'I will take whatever you think best,
And drain it, however deep it brim.'

On a road out of town, broken up, broken down,
Two covered the ground, slunk swiftly away.
And rebuked this ranger, this uninformed stranger,
Who asked what they whispered and said,
'Let me explain what the scriptures describe
About this Messiah'. Then they recognized
Him, in the breaking of bread.

And on Galilee's beach where they'd fled in the breach,
He came not to teach, but to feed them once more.
Not far from that spot, he had recently taught
Crowds that birds and lilies may
Eat and wear the choicest things,
His bread and fish on the fire
Assured them enough for today.

Contingency, Poems 1989-2001

FISHING OFF WARREN ISLAND

The cormorant on the last rock,
(High tide pinnacle of un-deluged stability)
Spreads its narrow wings to dry,
Holds the posture of stark helplessness
To absorb the sun.
The water runs from the veins of its pinions.
This act is necessary.
It is the required method for transformation
From driftwood, water, earth-locked looking
To ascending into sun-clear sky.
The dark form stretches on the rock,
Putting seas between the flooded fish
And the high heavens.
The fish-bird lifts a burden from me,
Its wings spread patiently against the pines.

STREET PEOPLE

If we keep our eyes high our vision will be sated
With insurance towers, where once there were steeples.
We will see the comforting works of our hands,
Where dust never settles and no man stands.
But on the pavement, in alleys, or grated
Heating vents, crouch the small street peoples
Grown all-important, blotting out success,
Challenging the interests which wear a vest.
They deeply disturb our utopian minds
For we cannot explain them, they make no sense
To worshippers of gross national product,
The standard of living in pounds and pence --
They thumb their grubby noses nicely
And declare we've miscalculated precisely.

James Howard Trott

THE FULFILLMENT OF DESIRE

Does the wind stop when it touches a tree?
Is the streambed dammed by a slender root?
Do tides touch sand and nevermore ebb?
Do calling birds mated grow mute?

Neither, my soul, can your eyes or ears,
Your touch, your thought, your imagination
Fulfill you in the leaves of desire --
But marks of eternal pagination.

Nothing short of stars is sufficient fire;
No one less than God fulfills desire.

PIÑATA

Who gave the little boys and girls
On earth making heavy weather,
Permission to beat me so,
Whirling at the end of my tether?

From my perspective,
I'd be best left alone.
I don't understand yours --
Can't prefer it to my own.

I am beaten, battered, broken in
Until little that was me remains intact.
I spin, toss, and am knocked back
Ready to spill all I've held within.

I can't stand it, not this sordid strife...

Do sweets pour from my broken life!

Contingency, Poems 1989-2001

DUST-UP

Wind off water stirred up dust,
Lifted and blew it with a whispered word,
Over the Garden and the earth through,
Squeezed one handful of dust into two.

But a sigh lisped from a misted tree,
"Be like the wind," the false breeze hissed;
And dust to dust tried and sinned:
Falling, settled, to elude the wind.

Wind came scouring, uncovered dust,
Gusted again when found dust cowering;
"Because of you cursed is the ground",
As dust sniffed, shifted dirt around.

To false wind-hiss from the tree
Wind spoke a curse something like this:
You poisoned dust; it will repay
Your licks with kicks 'til a fatal day.

Dust was driven out, yet offered hint
Of another day trust would be un-betrayed --
Wind come to earth, thorougher thrust
To beat the very sin from dust.

On dusty roads, trailing fingers in dust,
Until gathered for scattering on a tree he met
The false kiss-hisser. A last gasp he gave,
And blew his own dust out of the grave.

CYBERNETICS

The creation of a human steersman's realm
Proceeds on the assumption no one has the helm.

James Howard Trott

YESTERDAY'S SALT

Isn't yesterday's salt enough!
Haven't I lightened and leavened heaven's rising sufficiently
Without today being savory?
Lord, how I hate this antinomy
That when I have served best I must still serve thee.
I like to muse upon, to savor (that word again)
The fading grains of conversations past -- rather than fast
In order to prepare a sacrifice today of testimony ready always.
Can't my yesterday's wise advice, counsel and prayer
Suffice where I am fearful to fail?
Let me tally the tale, taste the fruit...
No, I don't suppose I want to be trodden underfoot.

GRAINS OF SNOW

Swirling between hourglass venturi walls of woods.
The grains of snow sound out an infinitesimal roar,
Like silence in a lonely room,
Rustling the still fallen leaves of time
In patterned patterned pulses
Too small to count, too many to measure,
Too steady to quite perceive.

Perhaps this is the rhythm of eternity.
Suddenly the world is white and we are wet,
And the bare woods are clothed again.

Contingency, Poems 1989-2001

THRESHOLD PAIN

The heartbeat builds as stretched lungs pump.
Thighs grow taught as shoulders slump.
Ankles ache and feet flop flat
As every nerve sings "enough of that!"
Threshold pain, a door to run through,
Seems like a wall or a grave to you,
But one that's faced, leaped over, passed,
By the athlete trained to run and last.

The fears build as memories surge,
Guilt swells up as instincts urge
Flight and escape, the ancient dread --
Rather than face it you're better off dead.
Threshold pain, a door to run through,
Seems like a wall or a grave to you,
But one you've passed a few times before --
Run to One who calls, called the Door.

The pressures build, as hostility grows,
Persecution breaks out, as the open foes
Of truth gain power, and color of law.
Believers turn, holding kings in awe.
Threshold pain, a door to run through,
Seems like a wall or a grave to the true,
But one that's passed by faith and grace --
In the power of one who's run this race.

HEAVEN IS A WINDY PLACE

Heaven is a windy place:
In every corner something moves --
Stirs, whirrs, or rushes outward
(Winds that strengthen, winds that sooth).

James Howard Trott

River breezes by the river,
Angels passing, horsemen flying
Stir the grass that feeds the lamb
That 'gainst the windblown mane is lying.

Heaven is a windy place
Sometimes you feel its wind on your face.

AROUND THE BLOCK
or
WITH A PILLOW OVER MY HEAD

One's fears are not one's favorite themes in poetry or song --
A poet hopes, a poet loves, a poet may doubt or long,
But fears, they say, are driving powers in my life and thine,
So I will list a fear or two, and acknowledge them mine.

I feared a girl who lived along my pathway to school.
She seemed to me an Amazon who once or twice, most cruel,
Beat me up, so I took a route around the block that passed
By her house for a year or so -- until return I dast.

I feared the dark, feared public gaze, feared ridicule or praise.
Feared friends and friendlessness alike, feared excitement or
    malaise.
I feared love and apathy, too much fun, no fun at all,
I feared to play or not play all games of skill or ball.

I feared my younger siblings, I feared cousins and aunts,
I feared the place in the attic I knew as a spector's haunts,
I feared what it was to be living, I feared to be dead,
At night I slept most soundly with a pillow over my head.

Contingency, Poems 1989-2001

HEROD'S WELCOME

What is the proper etiquette
For greeting a newborn child?
Pharoah commanded the midwives
To send each back whence he came.
Though contemporary doctors and judges
Don't bother to find out his name,
Herod at least asked the wisemen
To find that out if they could --
And then threw the same welcome,
Rolling out the carpet of blood.

'I DON'T CALL IT ANYTHING'

To insist upon a name is the prerogative of God.
No wonder now we so insist (fervently) in fraud
That we are he, each himself
(Likewise each to each)
And no divine prerogative beyond our wretched reach.

Yet silence becomes one who has no truth to say.

He is no tongue-tied fool who refuses to betray
The sure knowledge of his ignorance
By a guess or best try.
As well die for silence as flourish for a lie.

Let us, then, be thought less wise, let mystery abound --
To call something nothing may prove most profound.

James Howard Trott

OTHERS LIVES

"The tears of the sower and the songs of the reaper
Shall mingle together in joy bye and bye" – OLD HYMN

> We live each other's lives:
> Others our hopes fulfill;
> Others live out dreams and dreads
> We don't nor ever will.
>
> Some of the brightest visions
> And nightmares dark and long
> Are lived out by some other –
> His words to our song.
>
> We grudge sometimes the lives they lead;
> They lust for what we've done –
> Unless we learn all lives are loans
> Of another in whom they're one.
>
> Then we live for them this life our own;
> They theirs on our behalf;
> And toss up longing for another's lot
> As a thresher tosses chaff.

I WANT TO BE AT EVERYBODY'S PICNIC

> I want to be at everybody's picnic.
> Don't ask me why
> I sit and sigh
> And peer across the park
> From dawn to dark.
> I want to be at everybody's picnic.

Contingency, Poems 1989-2001

'SPOILED CHILD

The child is spoiled by something much more grim
Than pampering or protection -- too much given to him.
It is not too much too early, it's too little too late
That despoils a child -- None is spoiled by love too great.

THE LASER BEAM

The leper and the lazar more receptive to some power
Their fellows saw but dimly in reflection from clay,
A light-bolt like a laser beam, so direct they say
It will travel infinite time bright as the first hour,
Struck each at the infinitesimal atom-like seat of soul
And both rose up more than healed, transmogrified
Into persons wholly new, once corrupted (one had died)
They felt, heard, and saw: were made whole.

Thus around the lion-lamb, though all stand in praise,
But one at a time sees his face turned all ways;
Yet his laser beam light (that threw prophets down)
Will strike the heart of that mirror pure being
And at light speed reflect again each to each,
Thus light the whole cosmos with infinite seeing.

BABEL
(Victoria)

She speaks a few intelligible words among her prattling,
But mostly it's babble, despite the sound of sense.

She approximates (ninety-nine and nine tenths of the way)
The political leaders who lead us today.

Yet her babble is beautiful (theirs beneath comment).
She does not pretend to deceive -- herself or others,
But reaches toward content and form of sense

Whence she will attain by God's sustaining grace.
Babel in another place was heresy and destruction,
Yet "gate of God," in her it is better building --
Out of chaos into meaning like a spring tree greening
She passes -- through a gate indeed toward heaven.

LIDS AND LIPS

Close your eyes when there are things you should not see.
Close them when you should see things unseen.
God has given lids to the windows of the soul
So that we may close things in that keep us whole,
Or close the things out make the heart less clean.

Close your lips when there are things you should not say.
Close them when true speech would be in vain.
God has given bars to the all-defiling member
To lock in all its sparks, each world-lighting ember,
And to give his word the chance to sow its grain.

But open up your ears, you are made so much to hear:
There are voices high and low you ought to heed.
God has placed no shutters on the doorways of our hearts
So that we will quickly welcome what the still small voice
    imparts
And the neighbor who murmurs in his need.

Contingency, Poems 1989-2001

SIMON, THE BLIND MAGICIAN

Now blind, magician, renowned for my tricks,
    "the great power of God"
They called me, those back-hills hicks of Samaria.
    I was no fraud, then.
Yet when Philip came, I smelt power
    and believed his words of flame;
Underwent initiation, watched his art,
    labored to learn the Name.

Ah, but that was nothing, Philip's small skill,
    (They said he flew
Like a bird, but I never saw it), was but poor preview
    to the others,
Peter and John, true adepts, who then
    the Holy Ghost brought
And sharply rebuked me for asking
    if it could be bought.

I knew, in my heart of hearts, such powers
    were beyond money;
Came only to those who courted them with
    faithfulness, not sunny-day
Dedicates, but given heart and soul.
    So I studied the high truth,
And practiced self-denial, and dogged God,
    a spiritual sleuth.

I heard a tale strengthening my resolve,
    about a zealot muttering
Threats on all who served the Name, who was struck
    blind. And, stuttering,
Then gave himself to serve Whom he had persecuted,
    a zealot still,
Throughout the world, where much opposed he was
    impossible to kill.

James Howard Trott

Over the long years I listened and waited
    moving ahead with care,
Grown in repute for my small skills and wisdom,
    yet not for that rare gift:
The vision that knows and asks, and receives
    through the Risen,
With whom I was so familiar, yet who kept me
    as in prison,

For although I had seen and experienced
    his power's wide range
It remained beyond my grasp, still
    far remote and strange...
Until I gave up the alchemic search, the sorcerer's
    hope altogether,
And contented myself to climb for wealth and fame
    through time and weather.

I came at long last to Cyprus, where I entered
    the proconsul's favor,
Sergius Paulus, reputed wise, who indeed
    of savant had a savor.
He listened, I spoke of him called Christ (I was there
    known as Bar-Jesus),
And my place seemed made, there was talk of Rome,
    Caesar (and Croesus).

All that is gone, a harder fate overtook me
    there, a power forgot.
Paul, once blinded by the Jesus we speak of, came
    to court; we fought.
I lost -- not to subtlety, as I waged for
    the proconsol's mind...
No, I lost to raw power: the apostle
    struck me blind.

A blind magician, buyer of tricks, wishing
    once to manipulate God,

Contingency, Poems 1989-2001

This darkness has turned my ascendancy
    into evident fraud.
This humiliation, my eyes demise through the
    Only of Hebrew powers
Which I longed to know, to taste and hold,
    binds me in darkened hours.

I have power now and know, but possess it
    not as I thought it;
Not power to persuade or profit or turn -- what I thought
    when I would have bought it.
No, I have new power to see despite eyes
    that can't find the sun.
Un-magicked, I believe in the
    Uncontrollable One.

MIDNIGHT WAKING

    Though Freud may teach the opposites,
    It is more than theory where this papa sits
    To propose leading sons in midnight duties
    Compares at points to heaven's beauties.
    The Lord changes wet sheets and pants
    (Forgiving and healing circumstance)
    But also guides into better ways
    --Though he wake at midnight all our days.

CLOSED EYES

Our children in arms we feared to see their eyes dissolve,
Those great lucid lamps of light and love be shuttered,
And cease to signify.

James Howard Trott

Children, our own eyes were even more mysterious to us –
How they obliterated and created all reality
In a mere blink.

We fought the closing of our own, but found it harder
To accept the closing of others'.

No longer often in arms, we have learned to accept
The end of sight, life in shuttered dreams –
Accept, except . . .

When those we love close their eyes,
Those great lucid lamps of light and love
Which cannot cease to signify.

NAKED AND INSANE

The naked cross
After rending loss
Was stripped of its gloss
And went mad with grief.

The well-dressed tomb
In light-blotted gloom
Grew insane with rheum
And threw off its seal.

Around tombstones ran
The bold of the band
Seeking one dead man
Who lived they dreamed.

Against sepulchre whitening,
Shapes bright as lightning,
Apparitions frightening
To the heartsick seemed.

Contingency, Poems 1989-2001

Mad words they spoke,
Which like fever broke,
Spread among the folk,
Causing others to reel.

Then the warden of tears
Appeared, calmed their fears,
Who clothes who hears
In lucid belief.

THE HOSE NOT TAKEN

Two socks diverged in a yellow wash
And I, two-footed, gazed aghast,
Pondering where the other was,
One dark, cold morning, still unshod.

Then took the other, as just as fair,
But not sufficient, being sole,
Though as for that the passing there
Had worn in it a fair-sized hole.

And both that morning separate lay
In wool no foot had trodden black.
Oh, I took the one from my dresser drawer
And searched the corners one time more
For the other I distinctly lacked.

I will be saying this with a sigh
The day after washing for ages hence:
Two socks diverged in a yellow wash and I --
Put on one of a different dye
From another washday divergence.

James Howard Trott

STARE DECISIS

The old astrologers were starry deciders:
Analyzing what was fixed by fatal decree
As now our magistrates view high court decisions
And hand down the judgments on you and me.

But no star's so fixed God can't let it fall
Nor any judge so high God won't judge them all.

NO SPOILS

Good God, what can he mean!
After forty years, take no spoils!
What we got from Egypt has lost its charm,
Though not the memory how the outstretched arm
Of Pharaoh was shorter than Moses' staff,
How we danced by the flood.
How we did laugh!

But the Lord has some thought
To teach us something new, I think.
To have the victory but not despoil and loot
Here where milk and honey flow is perhaps new fruit
On the old tree of wisdom revealed
Which our own hopes of joy
Have thus far concealed.

We saw at Egypt and here again
Our little arms don't win the day,
Though a promised land we're to win and hold:
A people of faith, not hoarders of gold
Wrested from the world we're commanded.
Our witness is, in this further way
To serve barehanded.

Contingency, Poems 1989-2001

A SQUIRREL IN A TREE

No squirrel in a tree travels stem to stem,
Nor trunk to trunk, but scaling buttress boles,
Scrambles up along the limbs to branches smaller,
More diverse until he reaches peripheral twigs,
To which he barely clings, and from these jumps
To a neighboring fringe of small diffuse extremities
Thence either down or across and on.

The squirrel in a tree is a scientist, a theologian,
A practical theoretician clinging to what he learns,
And on his attainment of knowledge travels the forest.

I PRAY I WILL KNOW MY PISGAH

I pray I will know my Pisgah.
Oh Lord, though you make me a rover,
Let me know, like Moses,
When at last I can't cross over.

FREDDY

He always thought of others, he laughed with ease,
He once said, "I thank God for this disease."

At first he called it cancer, not afraid that we should know,
But doubting our reactions – he wondered if we'd go.

He had many friends, many willing to sacrifice,
But he wouldn't impose on anyone, was a little too nice.

So his last months were lonely as one usually thinks about it,
But he talked to heaven so freely perhaps they were crowded.

God's grace worked in him so that he used to inspire us--
God's grace which came to him by the agency of a virus.

Now Freddy is done, Fred is free,
Did far more than I for him for me.

CALLED OUT OF EGYPT

How fine it would be if geography were all it meant
To be sent from servitude to promised land,
From dark oppression to the golden strand.

How hard to receive when others leave, seem freed,
Go indeed to greener glens and plenitude,
Where none lacks for friend or food.

How distant seem the dales of dream, not dream but waking
Of at last forsaking this mud and straw,
This early death and foreign law.

How good the glimpse of pale palimpsest track
Reflected back between dusk and dawn
Through parted seas your people are on.

How stern the flames that burn in conscious heart
That none departs entirely Egypt here,
But none remains who counts her not most dear.

Contingency, Poems 1989-2001

THE OLD MAN
(A double-amputee in the nursing home)

Although I wondered, asked why,
The old man remained wry.
Half the man he used to be,
With twice the humor, that was he.
Nay, could never do more than complain by halves:
He lived, he died – no doubt he laughs.

TRANSLATOR

Borne across an inconvenience ---
Conceivably an insurmountable --
The man was lifted (men I should say):
Enoch, Elijah, before John.
And they in the flesh --
Not only in vision (as he and Paul).
John, by grace, was given back
To translate the inconceivable
Into Koiné Greek,
That others also might be borne across
The insurmountable inconvenience
Of not knowing the linguist as we should.
And while we await translation,
We each have brief passages assigned.

James Howard Trott

OUR WEARY HEADS

Our weary heads we bow before
Our head who bowed and bled for us.
We look upon the eyes divine
The eyes that shine, tears shed for us.

We raise our work-worn hands before
The hands that reached, nail-torn to us.
We look upon the arms spread wide
For us as Bride, cross-borne for us.

We open mouths to loose his praise
Whose mouth was struck, whose word us stays,
By whom all things that do exist
Were made, and in whom all that are made consist.

Our lungs suck breath for praises sung
To him whose poured life from his lungs,
Poured blood and water over death,
Rose up and sent eternal breath.

Through weary times, through times of pain,
Through scorn and sorrow, death and strain,
Each head-bowed body proffered is,
Receiving his, whose offered is.

HELEN LAUNCHED

Not a thousand ships, but a thin frail bark,
Not a grand passion, but a tiny dim spark,
Not out to long war, but in eternal surrender
Helen launched in light: solemn secret splendor.

Contingency, Poems 1989-2001

Helen B., once boisterous belle and beauty,
Loyal wife, faithful to friends and duty.
But the Helen we knew had become a frail thing
'Til her soul struck fire and set sail to sing.

She fought at last against bitterness, biting --
Friends become mean, and loved ones fighting,
'Til she'd nothing left of anger, self pity --
Nothing left to keep her in this world's city.

She beseiged a Troy greater far than Greece,
Armed herself, 'til Hector's crew looked mere geese.
She found surer hiding than a Trojan horse,
And launched homeward on a surer course.

THE POET AS ALCHEMIST
(for Robert Duncan)

Waving my yellow wand I make gray marks, ashes not sparks --
No alchemist so poor, though few did more.
Nevertheless, I profess poetry to be a kind of alchemy.

The alchemist gives himself to recipes, to chemistries,
But also fashions his retort (for life is short)
Refining his vessels and his fires, as he aspires...

So poets, though in reverse process: they seek success
At turning dross back into gold, the hot to cold,
And riches out of melted lead, in heart's heat, still head.

Untarnishable metal is a high endeavor, achieved never
Or if momentarily attained, never sustained --
For both alchemists' and poets' lusts (acids) rust.

James Howard Trott

Sublimity, for all the cant, no matter how scant,
Is a longing rooted in our being, just beyond seeing --
Spurs seeking and reaching, more than poetry or preaching.

The brief palimpsests, gold specks glimpsed test
The alchemist's fear, that all gold he sees here
May be but an elation of his peculiar imagination,

And lead still to all others -- so his poet brothers,
This logic of the soul (psychology) most fear, hold dear
The hope their blendings and fusions are not illusions.

Theirs is a forbidden art, though fashion recasts the censor's part,
But mankind as always was, the forbidden does;
Though seldom men know it, as well as alchemist or poet.

He forges and forms his tools, this one purpose rules:
This purpose, and this alone, to find the philosopher's stone,
To at last achieve, nor fail, in quest of the grail...

Which is not only an heirloom or token, of past bounds broken,
But the means of achieving yet, what no one will forget,
Gold out of baser metals, peace out of what unsettles.

Thus bending his will the sage arrives at a certain age,
Where he dimly remarks (not sure for he's already embarked
Upon the world's end's sea) that he cannot cease to be,

Cannot stop bellows pumping, nor stay heart from jumping,
Nor put out fire in forge, nor drop the Olympian torch,
Nor hold back associations, nor subtle integrations . . .

So that everything that comes to hand, tumbles into the can --
Everything: food, garbage, thought, all felt, seen, taught,
As well all passions, and all beloved – Oh, Midas the gold you
    covet!

All welded together, heaps of mud out of this anti-Midas flood --
Nothing quite gold, but all fired. Nothing true but all inspired.

Contingency, Poems 1989-2001

Dimly, then, he suspects it sad he may be nearly mad --

This, though leaden, soon molten. He speculates if it's golden
And immersed in his mind's *aqua regia*,
Precipitates this thought before amnesia:

Is poetry alchemy? Have they ever been?
Have I lived in illusion
 . . . Or perhaps in sin?

THE RIGHT SORT OF BANG

On Independence Day, that rite when we most rely,
Most depend on the accounts and pride of invisible fathers;
There are many conundrums for those who are brave-hearted,
Independent and God-fearing enough to ask them.
The starkest and most difficult of questions are those
Shot from the dim hedges of little boy minds
About what to do with this year's firecrackers.
Many minor rites revolve about these small munitions --
Mother's stern warning about lost fingers and eyes,
Dad's marvelous wisdom in coming up with
New forms of cannon or demolition demonstration.
The central questions remain, however, when the boy stands
With a braided-fuse pack or two of crackers, his own --
And no more.
 It is a stark question I say and do not apologize,
Because there are really two options, only two,
And others but variations on a theme.
Either he may hoard and fire them one by one,
Or light the whole pack into one glorious uproar.
This is the question every small boy asks upon waking
Every independent day.

James Howard Trott

SECOND BEST

The loveliest girl in the class has no rival, unless
It be the second best, who fighting for social survival,
Constantly puts to test the claimant's title.

The most popular politician cannot lose, albeit
As pundits see it, a dark horse may make news
And somehow suddenly become the image voters choose.

Speaking of horses, or athletes or racers, cars,
While proven stars are favored often, their pacers
May overrule the czars, shoot from second to first placers.

More sure than any struggle over beauty, power, speed
God promises to lead his bride to his best for her dower.
Yet she must heed, not build barns or towers.

The outcome of God's struggle with sin is sure, set,
But beware who bet on the church's wisdom, her
Propensity continues yet second best to prefer.

NO RUNT IN THE LITTER

Rural wisdom has little room for the ugly debate
Waged by urban philosophers about death as fate
Rightfully considered as the prerogative of men,
To be decided democratically and administered when
Convenient to the greater happiness of others,
(The recipient assumed glad to so serve his brothers.)

Contingency, Poems 1989-2001

Although tales of bare survival are frequently told,
No rural sage, though his tales make blood run cold,
Draws the point that mankind lives like a crowd in a boat,
Where some must drown so some may float.

No, the rural sage's stories include parts where men fail,
Men fall, and feel hemmed in, or maybe short of bail.
But men are together, be the battle ever so bitter.
None cast out, none abandoned – no runt in the litter.

SEMI-PRIVATE HELL WITH DETACHED BATH

>Two months rent deposit,
>No children or pets,
>Well-maintained, coal-heated --
>Here nobody forgets
>His key or her bill --
>Management does the math:
>Every upwardly mobile soul seeks
>A private hell -- with detached bath.

DERELICT

Stale alcohol, holey clothes, two days growth, an emaciated face;
Loneliness, a back alley bed, oblivion, universal disgrace;
Family, job, friends lost through dereliction of duty;
Appearance, acts, words declaring nothing of truth or beauty:

He has abandoned all. Nothing remains to him except the odd
Incarceration, violent fears, sweats, crying out to God.
He seems to believe in something pious citizens call heretic:
Despite all cost, there's some duty he will not derelict.

SING ME

>Sing me to yourself, Lord,
>Tune my heart and mind.
>Make me a song.
>Take me for a sign
>Of your great lordship
>Over every rock and hill --
>And when they crumble --
>Mumble me still.

FOXFIRE

The blue light on the forest floor at dusk-done dark
Invisible to lamplit eyes
Is foxfire, the unburnt brand's cool and living spark,
That dimly sends it steady sign
Beyond the mixed woods towers.

"Live coal" we say -- but this lives indeed,
As heaven's angels beside the one of light
Whose angry glow will at last expire
While theirs radiates eternal fire.

A living light we see barely if at all,
This "false fire," *faux* fire, foxfire looms

Contingency, Poems 1989-2001

Up in the darkness only when ones eyes see the glooms;
Adjusted to the reality of night, acquired sight
Capable of apprehending by vision and yearning
What eyes corners discern but not quite.

Then foxfire shines brightly -- no illusion,
No effort to see, with a kind of majesty --
Inspiring awe in ancient Greeks, Germans, Latins,
Henry David Thoreau, and English poets,
Who know it more than natural phenomenon.

It is a signal sent among the trees,
To men seeing others as these at first,
Half-blind, but now becoming clearer,
The light is dearer because it portends,
Blends truth with light and lives and tends
To fool us, fox us, and lives amidst decay,
And though we don't see it, won't go away.

HEAVEN DROPPED THE BABY

Even before mankind formally declared itself God
And approved the murder of babies, especially before birth,
There was occasional cause to consider divine love fraud,
Fair excuse to doubt grace ran things on earth.

Every time a baby died, before or after delivery,
Doctors looked helpless and ministers got shivery.
"Higher purpose" and "divine plan" rang a little hollow,
And arguments syllogistic got a bit hard to follow.

The one apologetic that seems to console toward hope,
Aside from raging or despair, or alcohol or dope,
Is that God became a man and felt as we do maybe,
When he himself was born, and himself the dropped baby.

James Howard Trott

YOU CAN GO HOME AGAIN

You <u>can</u> go home again, you whimper-stamping sinners --
The old home, the old home town, are all too there and staid.
It's some reverse hometown, some vision of utopia
Makes eternal places here and roots easily extricated.
Truth is, earth's all transient : the fixed as well as the mobile;
The ninety year in one spot as well as one in ninety.

You just aren't so heroic, so larger than the life of places --
That your wandering squandering put you out of village graces.
The only home you can't go back to is the one you refuse –
Certain! None's dragged to reunions who wants to be excused.

THE FOOLISH THINGS TO CONFOUND THE WISE

        The foolish live and preach
        In such strange guise
        That, lo, their lives and sermons
        Confound the wise,
        Who being confounded,
        Become themselves fools
        To preach back to the proud new wise --
        Dual tools --
        Ore crumbling against ore,
        Siren singing against siren.
        Always heated by one forge,
        Iron shapes iron.

Contingency, Poems 1989-2001

SQUIRREL SHADOW

My life has turned a corner
Like the brick-backed shadow
Of this squirrel running a wire --
It accelerates suddenly --
And as quickly diminishes.
Yet this is but the shadow
Of the narrow-pathed squirrel,
Getting where he wants to go.

WOODS INTO WINTER NIGHT

Needles of dusk scatter
Lost in the haystack of woods.
Cold-crackled leaves disintegrate
In the falling of light.

A spectre of spectrum,
Unconscious rainbow, fades from
Pale red horizons
To pale violet heights.

The black and bowing
Tree priests sway
And shake interceding hands
Their prayer roars on into night --

The interlacing fingers
Of the distant sky
And darkening woods
Close tapered and tight.

Then moon rises among treetops
As fine as frost
And trees but tremble
Where formerly they tossed.

STEP OF FAITH

When the blind man came to the intersection
There was silence all about.
But when after seemed ages, someone spoke,
"It's green for you" – he stepped out.

WHEEL WEIGHTS

The tractor puts it hand to plow,
It's wheels never turning back.
Yet tug of plow against the earth
Demands more than it has at birth.

Therefore wise farmer by mechanic means
Loads the wheels with great weights cast,
Bolted and welded to the wheels' hubs
By hammered force to make them fast.

By these burdened, much weighed down,
It plows down deep where seeds are sown.

Contingency, Poems 1989-2001

STILL LIFE

The bananas in a basket
No longer in bunches,
But made singular
By seven year old Jed -- curiously --
With the morning sunlight
Burnishing just the backs of them,
Turning them almost translucent.

USEFUL STUFF

Two garages, two basements
And an attic at least
He's filled with things
That grow like yeast.

It might prove useful
This behemoth bric-a-brac
If it doesn't break his
Heart, mind or back.

THE SWIFT

That thin-bodied bow-winged flicker of feathers,
Twinkling and twittering, never seeming to rest,
Soars and sails and speaks itself swift.
Swift it is, yet never the short way --
The proverbial straight line between two points --
This bird is ours.

James Howard Trott

Like a bat out of hell it flitters at dusk
In flocks of feeders on invisible insects.
Its wings are erratic, seem to alternate flight --
Illusion right knows not what left is doing.
Bat-like it nests in dark caverns of chimneys
Or hollow trees, brooding in bleakness --
These birds like us.

Its tiny claws, four toes forward, are hidden away --
Family Apodidae: those with no feet,
Stranger, alien, obscure seeker --
Seeking some means of alighting, a rest
Not just a season between furnace or winter's blast
-- Somewhat like you.

Science says swift asleep in its nest
Adapts body heat to shifting seasons --
Becoming all things to all times --
Does not fight the hot or cold,
But saves its strength for the suffering of soaring
-- Ah, bird! Come swift for me.

TWO KINGS WEPT

Seated on a high white marmoreal throne,
Xerxes wept great streams of tears ---
Not at defeat, no loss of his own,
But over the evanescent years
Brought before his heart's minds' eye
By the Persian parade there marching by.

Artabanus, wise uncle, adviser unmatched,
Remarked the contrasting conditions, response:
Xerxes first power on earth then watched
That embodiment, which great Hellespont

Contingency, Poems 1989-2001

Had just crossed, and in but a few weeks,
Was expected to bring to submission the Greeks.

Jesus seat was no white throne when
He sat on a hill and wept like a mother.
He reviewed the people of Jerusalem
And mourned the knowledge which no other
Of us can see with eyes of heart or mind:
How to lose for the lost what he founded to find.

Artabanus gave comfort (none could comfort Jesus)
By assuring Xerxes there are things worse than death,
Proof being how living man sometimes seizes
And proclaims a preference for grave to more breath.
He went on to claim the god this gift gave
Envies us our escape to the grave.

Christ mourned and none could reinterpret
His sorrow in terms that would ease his grief,
For he'd already traded his white throne set
On highest hill, for immortal relief
Of mankind forfeit of any grave escape
Except what his unrelieved sorrow could shape.

THE TANK

When we enter this jail we're thrown in the tank,
Regardless of crime or connection or rank,
Where some stand, some sit on the concrete floor,
As some complain less and others more.
Some light up, others bum a smoke
As someone cracks a jailhouse joke.
Some silent, pray; some silent, no more;
Some listen carefully at the door
For steps or news or a familiar voice.

James Howard Trott

When lunch is brought in, few rejoice.
Some come from court bearing a sentence,
Others hope their new-found repentance
Will soften the judge's stony heart,
Others know to play the well-worn part.
Some go from here to a narrow cell,
Others leave for a world never loved so well.

TEACHING CREDENTIALS
(On a thought from Steve Osborne)

The inscrutable geniuses cannot teach,
Are puzzled by nothing but human reach.
We need, we seek, we believe God lent us
The nincompoop, the non compos mentis,
The ignorant rube who struggled, slipped,
Over every rough spot where others tripped
In this disordered world, our school,
Where ease is rare, and failure the rule.
Find the one experienced in how to make
Every error, his degree in Mistake:
That man's your teacher, tempered by test,
Like us all ways tempted, compassioned and best.

TWO DAY STORM DURING HARVEST

Do not send grace when we are bent
Upon our labors, Lord, repent you now
Your awful raining on these fields
Which do but suffer, lose their yields.
We would work, we would gather;

You might have done this earlier, rather --
Watered well our seed when sown
In the thaw, not now, with rain wind-blown
Soaking standing straw of stunted grain;
It's so useless now, Lord -- try again.
Often thus your clock goes wrong --
The right tune to an awkward song.
You do not seem to ken the measure
Of our dance, nor know our pleasures, pain
Aright. You who should, since fully man
As well as God. Please attend to our plan!

ALPHA AND OMEGA

We are always beginning and always about to make an end,
While you came the end of the beginning,
The initiation of the conclusion,
Z to our A, infinity to our one:
Therefore our bewilderment.

Alpha is a great undertaking, experiment, first discovery,
The first mumbled, scribbled effort of the Greek youngster
At organized thought, universal communication, toward truth.

Omega is a seal, a finale, the last syllable before the sigh
Which says I've done it, I've learned, something's complete.

And whether it's A, alpha, aleph, or Japanese "ah"
Or zed, omega, tav or "wa", there is a pre-Babel unity
Of sense and feeling about our learning.

But none of us learns A first of all. Something precedes:
Be it Mama, Baba, or Haha. Likewise, learning the alphabet
Is only a beginning, Z is no end:

James Howard Trott

Great struggles follow: words, orthography, spelling,
    grammar
Logic, and rhetoric -- or sorry pseudo-science.

None of us, save our madman, calls himself first or last.
We hold it a high insult to say someone thinks himself
The end all and be all.

We excuse old tales that start, "In the beginning..."
As we excuse others starting, "Once upon a time...".

When we entertain respectable thoughts about God, even as
    Creator,
We do not give serious room to the idea you <u>were</u>
Before everything else. In our heart of hearts we suspect you
    evolved, too.

And the inescapable effrontery of your words on the cross
Blasts across our interminable universe: <u>it is finished</u>!

TO DONKEYS EVERYWHERE

To you pigheaded sons who won't do your math,
And you stubborn daughters who follow other drummers,
And you stiff-necked men who take on all comers,
And you hard-nosed ladies who will not be moved :
Your recalcitrant qualities have often proved
The same character of the burden's beast
Who carried the load and often the scorn,
Like the donkey who journeyed before Christ was born.

Was it also a donkey's colt that before the feast,
Carried the Lord amidst hosannas and palms,
Soon turning to "crucify," thus men change psalms?

Contingency, Poems 1989-2001

And wasn't it a donkey with God's truth in its bray,
Though beaten and cursed, halted in the way
When it saw God's angel blocking Balaam's path?

A THIN TUNE

To pipe a thin tune on a dreary day,
Having come away from the anthems of choirs,
Having carried a part with swelling heart --
Now that all past (but an interlude
As when smiles intrude on a solemn feast).
My voice seems least -- discordant, awry:
My principle task but to hum and remember,
Or hope December shall some day be May.

The kingdom comes imperceptibly -- they say,
But always to stay. How is it then
So much fades among men -- the best and the least,
The hunger and feast, lending undue credence
To the myths of heathens that there spins a wheel
Like a spinners creel, around and around
With no new sound, no end, no end,
And no true friend?

Lord, still I pipe thin tunes to thee
And see, this, Lord, my halting dance --
No waltz, no measured step, but a clog,
A faltering step, a tumble, a slog, a step
Along a road out of celebration into winter's day,
Out of the feasthall into the freezing.
Yet to be a pleasing sacrifice,
I would sleep on dune or ice,
And hear at my funeral but a thin-piped tune.

James Howard Trott

TO ALL THE SECRET CELIBATES

To all the secret celibates, we honor and we praise you
For rocking on their baseless stands
The clayfoot gods whose faith demands
Obeisance to each sexual twinge
No matter how it might unhinge
Civilized world or civil soul;
You keep the flame, you keep us whole,
We praise you.

TIME IN THE ATTIC

The speed of living or the speed of trying mars so much,
In our hasty village, excludes so much from ordinary life
That was other-times precious, memorialized dying,

Which our trivial living makes almost inconsequential:
Nothing is revered when no one's reverential or pauses
To consider the possibility that past things matter.

So that now we scatter and know no ancient dwellings,
Once every seven years say the broadcast statistics,
Perfect peripatetics, with nothing in our attics.

In the past, yes, in my past, too, I admit it,
The attic was the family museum, the archaeological midden
Where were hidden all manner of ancient curios and idols,

Clothes, a dried rose, books with strange titles and photos
Of obscure gatherings in outlandish dress, furniture, broken bits
Of things one can't guess and these we'd sort through.

Not weekly or monthly, but sometimes yearly we'd spend time,
Time in the attic both to know more clearly what was there,
But also to clear the air, in our own dusty minds,

Usually in the spring and the fall, never summer's heat.
These transition times seemed best for the task never complete
Of sorting, compiling, reminiscing through trunks.

Perhaps its a small loss that attics have receded from life,
No longer needed; that we're better at throwing things away,
Perhaps that's why poetry, too, seems to have had its day.

TEARS OF SOWING

    The tears of the sower
    Flow no slower
    For the bruises and shocks
    Of the roots and rocks --
    But shoots to stalks
    Like the dream of a sleeper
    Are kept by the keeper
    As songs for the reaper.

THE HEAVENLY CITY

    Abounds with the color, and smells and sounds
    Of every tribe and every tongue. The young
    Exchange and blend, no new friend foreign,
    None strange. Each belongs, knows new songs.

James Howard Trott

Commerce bursts from each shop and store,
From dawn each door, a gate, admitting,
Providing and fitting, decking, adorning,
No need scorning, no want permitting.

Streets speed soul and substance through space,
In rambling race. Each finds his own pace,
None time wastes, but deliberately hastens,
In intricate parade, conveyed to his place.

Clean as the hour after downpour gusting,
Safe as houses of stone and brick,
Quiet as the wee hours short. Vital
As sparrow flock in concrete court.

SWITCHBACKS

The traveler scales the higher ridge
By no straight way of ascent.
Narrow indeed may be the path,
But back and forth it's bent --
A wending way, a zigzag road,
A switchback trail he traces.
He has no simple compass point,
To keep his feet in his high places.
If bearings there be, then these are two --
A pair the upward traveler hath:
The first, the downward magnet of sin;
The second, true north, with faith the path.
Repentance, to the left, from sin a back-bearing,
Praise, to the right, both by true pole faring.
This road is hard-cobbled with cancelled debt,
Dropped by others gone higher yet.

Contingency, Poems 1989-2001

TO A CHILD LEARNING TO DIVE

The evolutionary myth disserves you again:
Having gotten over the initial excuses
That you are afraid of the water,
That it's cold, that you might drown,
And having learned to jump feet first,
You must now turn up-side-down.
No gradual progress from here to there is known.
The attempts to rationalize the plunge
With middle ways have all failed.
From head-up vertical to feet-up vertical
Must be done in the air --
Hitting the water horizontal is nowise recommended
For it hurts, and may discourage you
From ever diving at all.
Abandon your life-loving attitude
And hit the water up-ended.
Our limitations drive us to acts of faith:
Because of our fetters, we fly.

SPRING IS NOT AS WARM

When the conceptual sun first touches our skin, not light but heat,
We barely recall how to respond, we've missed the beat
Of his rays too long, nor do we recognize these things
He brings, grass, leaves, and flowers, these seasons called springs.
And as in many another case of sudden, immediate love,
We overestimate the strength in these caresses from above,
Which do not keep off wind's chill, nor touch us in the shade,
So our tendency to under-dress with bad colds is repaid.
Thus the first tastes, first touches of other joys
May seem in hindsight like the practical joke that annoys
One, especially when played by a friend. Our own haste
Sets us up to feel robbed of a feast, once we've had a taste.

That full joy we anticipate we'll know when we meet it,
Though spring is seldom as warm as our hearts heat it.

UNDERGOING PRIVATION

To be lonely one need not be Robinson Crusoed,
Or becalmed and Ancient Marinered on a plague-swept sea.
Americans, for instance, are lonely and think it normal.

Born out of surging independence, pride
In distance from the nearest friend, and fiestiness,
Our nation leads in the rhetoric of mutuality
And the furthest removes of isolation.

What is privacy but the state of deprivation?
What is independence but a self-sufficient lie?
Where are we going as people, as a nation,
Undergoing privation until we die?

SILENCE SENDS MESSAGES

Silence sends messages
Surcease of speaking sounds,
Loud rebounds the signal sense:
No answer whispers "listen".

Contingency, Poems 1989-2001

THE WAITING ROOM

We would not have met,
Would not have gathered there,
Except that your arrival
Was imminent -- by air.

SEARCHING THE STONES

I stop beside the road --
I take my rest.
I look for stones amongst, amidst
The stones I search.
I seek the ones,
The one that stands,
I seek amidst these gravel grains,
Significant,
A crystal of truth
I do not know --
Nor can describe --
May know it when
I find it.

VEHEMENCE

What to do with vehemence?
Nico it? Pickle it?
Or fickle crowd-wise tickle it?
Stifle it and salvage sense?
Engrave, entomb it thus
-- and whence?

James Howard Trott

POLITICAL ECONOMICS

    If I had a nickel
        And you had a dime
            I'd give you a quarter
                To trade me for mine.

SAVE OR SPEND

Granddaughter of Liberty, mother of us all,
She occupies a double room in a residential hall,
And pipes her tiny tune to her heart's failing drums
"I can save it or I can spend it," for anyone who comes.

She is not non compos mentis, not senile or insane --
This is not her only word, but her regular refrain --
Left alone with nothing else to occupy her soul
She meditates upon the things formerly her goal.

She is grandmother of us all, daughter of the free,
Distracted like her forebears by dilemmas of the rich:
To spend or to save -- which is liberty?
To have her cake or eat it, to scratch or to itch?

She is Miss Poor America, despite how we pretend it,
She has very little left – to either save it or spend it.

Contingency, Poems 1989-2001

THE WEDDING REHEARSAL

We follow these instructions though they fall so dry
On ears expecting something high and glorious.
We take our positions, stalk our steps,
After entering, turning -- and learn to recite
According to the willed and written rite.
We muff some lines, we stumble, we joke,
Laugh at each other, and feel the weight of time.

Only the central pair act as though they see
Beyond this thin part-hearted show;
The bride and the groom almost seem to dance
To the fullest chords, pomp and circumstance of tomorrow,
When actor-words become star-ringing acts,
Beginnings (and ends) merged in living facts.

Most of us yawn and shift, wishing to be done,
Anxious for the dinner promised after this dry run --
This rehearsal which often seems more death than life,
Except to the two who grow man and wife.

WORSHIP DANCERS

You beauties of the living God
Who turn both eye and toe,
Who lift your arms and hands and wings,
Your faces from below,
Which blush at once from calling-pride
And humility of place,
Oh, Dance your hearts as well as feet
Partner our souls with grace.

James Howard Trott

Your hands turn ever in your task,
Your fingers curl and spread
To grasp the insubstantial things --
Like angels at your heads, whose
Voices only you can hear, singing
God's truth through mutes.
The strains our longing ears receive
Play from lithe limbeck lutes.

You lead us praising God by sight
Where eyes can never soar.
You teach our spirit legs their part,
The movements of the cosmos start
To be our own steps' score.
For as desire is drawn out chaste,
You show our heart-feet how to haste
Nor step nor gesture ever to waste
On this broad world's brief floor.

PROPHETIC UTTERANCE

If your stomach gets fluttery,
And your bowels turn buttery,
As your lips become stuttery,
You've found her.

PRESENT FAITH

The present time
Like an unmatched rhyme
Binds my will to pantomime.

Contingency, Poems 1989-2001

I cannot guess
What dream or duress
Emerges next to bleed or bless.

If the moment's the key
To eternity,
Someone much quicker
Must steal it for me.

ANGELS OF PROMISE AND DOOM

The angels who came to Abram with the promise
Wended their way to Sodom with its doom.
Not all his rhetorical efforts
Or compassion dispelled the gloom
Hanging sulphureous over the cities of the plain,
Soon to be distilled in destruction and pain.

Dual citizens find it hard at that final hour
Decreed by cities for deciding which to shun;
To claim the other, embrace it's rights and power:
To separate to integrate, to be torn into one.
So we citizens of a nation dark death shrouded
Mourn and argue with God, be it ever so beclouded.

But whence from hence we know not,
Ninevah or Gomorrah, tomorrow.
Can his distant promises suffice
To assuage our brooding sorrow?

James Howard Trott

PORTABLE DUNGEON

The bars of memory
On windows and doors
Are bitter steel,
Are concrete floors
Sealing us in,
From fear, and doubt,
And the unforgiven --
So we never get out.

THE EXECUTIONER
(Grace Upon Waking)

He leads the man, the old man
Out, out of bed, out of camp,
After the cock crows every morning.

Hangs him on a scaffold, on a gibbet
As a scoundrel, a traitor,
For a clear public warning.

PHAROAH'S BUTLER AND PHAROAH'S BAKER

Both Pharoah's Butler and Pharoah's Baker
Told their dreams to a Servant of their Maker.
Joe told the Butler, your dream of the cup
Means your head will be lifted up.

Contingency, Poems 1989-2001

Then said the Baker, tell me mine,
Seeing you can interpret so fine.
Joe said dreams aren't jokes, don't scoff --
It turns out yours will be lifted off.

ARK ON THE PLAINS

The dry-land farmer (like Noah) counts for gain
On the unlikely chance of a good long rain.

ARREST

I should not be here. I perform the duty of temple guards
Who duty refuse -- who approach seldom and only
To arrest me. God, I feel lonely! Hear me, father,
If the cup can pass... whose feet lead through the grass?

It is Judas -- predicting betrayal hurt less than the fact:
Watching trust fail before me, I am passive to his kiss,
I know now I must walk the whole long road to do this,
The task appointed me, but lo -- how the others react!

This my arrest, then, is a watershed, a winnowing.
I alone am left, even now a widowed king,
This scourging, this mocking seem small to compare
With the loss of love -- the double-cross I bear...

Alone ... but I am not alone, not yet, and then but a time
Condensing all believer's eternity of hell, but I'm

James Howard Trott

Ready now for that, for I've tasted the option,
Dutiless, careless, loveless men -- I'll buy their adoption.

And helpless, I will help more than ever they did or could,
Broken I will bind up as no doctor would
Heartlessly killed, I revive and un-harden.
Arrested and punished, I will free and fully pardon.

PERPETUAL

The sign says "Lots for Sale -- Perpetual Care".
It gives one a warm feeling -- knowing those who lie there
Will never be neglected, though all kindred should die;
Surely this confidence is no pie in the sky!
If the only immortality is that of a name,
Then the care of that stone is essentially the same
As eternal life, and we do well to invest
In our own small mansion in the plot of the blessed.

INFORMATION REVOLUTION
(Inspired by advertisement in "evangelical" magazine
for computer that will find texts for sermons)

The data which falls on good ground --
He having ears indeed hears --
Will bring forth fruit a hundred fold,
Though it were sown in tears.
But that on hard disc only
Or choked by mere science' success,

Contingency, Poems 1989-2001

No information revolution
Can reach to water or bless.
Blessed are the feet and mouth
Of him who weathers the techno-drouth.

THE PAINTED TREES

The crimson powder of the ancient strumpet
Brushes the disapproving trees,
Their hypocrisy declared as loud as a trumpet,
For they, too, dying, live to please.
In the hallowed tent of the maple at noon
Blood tells glory, "too soon, too soon."

THE BACHELOR'S BOWL

If your burning desire is to be more holy than humble,
Then with me, you find frequent cause to grumble
Over heaven's failure to perform as advertised --
Seldom to clean as thoroughly of earthly hurley-burley
As in expectations we've prized.

Bachelors keep house in just this limited sense
That they clean only when there is offense.
They wash or sweep, otherwise act Levit-ious
Only on those occasions when they fear the invasions
Of friends more fastidious; or more compelling
Than this is, a bachelor does his dishes
When none can be found to serve his wishes.

James Howard Trott

We are vessels piled in a bachelor's sink.
He is concerned that we're crusty and stink
Not on principle, or in order to reduce
The mess in the way or the threat of decay,
But rather because he would prepare us for his use.

OWING TO WHAT

In a materialistic world
All manner of owing
Is ultimately to the atom
Which keeps us all going.

The macrocosmic mirror
Magnifying minisculities;
Makes us slaves to house and car,
Subject to their cruelties.

To be unpossessed by possessions,
Unconsumed, not bound to consume,
Is possible only among the few
Who find all owing to <u>whom</u>.

HOW ART THE FALLEN MIGHTY

"How art the mighty fallen," judge the high
And mighty confident of our tenacious hold on this precarious
    nest
(This tower of the blessed), we ponder and pedantically correct

Contingency, Poems 1989-2001

Those whose wings are wrecked, whose wax waned in
 weakness,
Whose loss in the aerial Preakness our sympathies but sigh.

But our ordered bench reels, and all untidy
Tips dangerously, leaving us shocked when failures, new-
 fledged,
Rise from depths they've dredged, begin to lift, then soar,
(As they've no right any more) and turn and scale the sky
Untouched by such as you (or I). How art the fallen mighty!

OPENING OTHERS PRESENTS

Those family films captured in eight millimeter,
Several moments long, at Christmas and birthdays,
Are disconcerting among their enchantments,
For often I have seen ambered therein --
Firstborn person, what I know of sin.
I could not wait for brothers, sister
To open their gifts, always gave a hand.
Greedy impatience for more chances to covet?
Groping, controlling, idiosyncrasy?
The wish to end suspense, restore order?
Or was I already trying to be God?

PART FOR WHOLE

Some of us do it without ever considering, oblivious
To what we do as well as the reasons behind, pay no mind
(Having little to spend) ((do I offend?))
(((Emerson said consistency is a hobgoblin to us))).

James Howard Trott

We substitute the part for the whole, with no goal,
But psychological protection: the infection of imagination
With panicky panoramas, vast and infinitesimal dramas,
Acknowledging which taxes too much toll.

We grasp at comprehensible bits in starts and whatever fits
Our little logics and lores, our raggedy stores
Of small experience, minor memories and readings,
Our own special pleadings where our own judgment sits.

Those of us whose small worlds label us intellectual
Argue that as definers, we are purifying refiners;
Like jewelers, cut great gems into small clear apothegms,
Limiting our scope and reach in order to be effectual.

While those living believing among us, consciously religious,
Cannot long stand overwhelming demand to live by faith:
Turning to seen formulae, liturgies, office, personalities,
Trusting in verities most measurable and prestigious.

God is not subject to our little measurements, divisions,
Nor offers us small closed rooms in which to dwell.
The incomprehensible is a large part of our provisions --
The only lasting little haven is called hell.

ON THIS WET MORNING

The offering that rises from the wet prairie
Floods whole fields into fertile fathoms.
Sweet, wholly good, rich with almonds, raisings.
It is a dessert smell, an undeserved mercy,
A surprise, relief and respite.
We are this much more likely to harvest abundance.
We cannot work in the fields today.

Contingency, Poems 1989-2001

The sun which drove us on
And wilted the grain-heads is hidden.
But more and over and beyond
The smell of rain on earth and grass
Is its own reward, and essence and assurance.

BURGLAR'S FINGERPRINTS

A burglar visited our new old home
We had moved in but two months since.
He tried our doors and windows and all,
Left on one a fine set of prints.

Someone's been trying the doors once again,
Trying the sashes, entry his goal.
I've seen the signs, the marks of the hands
Of the burglar who pries at my soul.

ON REFLECTING
On Saint Boniface

If many a Germanic heart was pierced
With woe at the fall of Wodan
When the fay one felled his tree,

What woe Christian has come to thee
Who thyself are felled and thy God silent --
The kingdom taken by the violent?

James Howard Trott

CHEWING DIAMONDS

Chewing diamonds, crystalline truth
Stronger than jaw or tongue or tooth --
A stream of bright spikes, spectacular:
Awful aliments, original, oracular.

To a throat used to gruel,
To a stomach stuffed with starch,
This meal of shining burning is cruel,
An ice blizzard in March.

Can my molars and eye-teeth survive it --
Can my entrails hold adamants in?
Or will they pierce and kill me --
Grave stones engraving within?

And yet, this meal over which I mutter
Converts my soul to a diamond cutter!

THE OCCASION OF A POEM

I mark the occasion of a poem by rising early from bed,
By calling a convocation of heart and hand and head
To plan the festivities, to invite all the right guests
To think about the seating, all conjunctions to bless,
New associations started and old ones refreshed, renewed,
That none should remember it too rowdy or subdued.
Many the gifts and condiments to be acquired procured,
All the special obligations and music to be assured.
Some will feel awkward, uneasy, unless we show 'em,
How fine the celebration on the occasion of a poem.

Contingency, Poems 1989-2001

THIS IS A DESERT PLACE
AND NOW THE TIME IS FAR PASSED
(Mark 6:35)

That, Lord, is the moan of my malaise,
Those words, that fact.
A dimly lit burnt over waste,
Death Valley at dusk.

It is! It is!
Is it, Lord?

And although there is no hope,
We can at least cut our losses,
Act with some dignity
In our everlasting hunger,
And go somewhere out of
Each other's sight to starve.

Don't string me out, string us out,
String them out any further, Jesus.
Send us away!

Desert, Lord, the time all passed.
What was of abundance,
What was of opportunity
--Gone.

It is, isn't it...
No, no, don't confuse the issue with particulars!
No, kid, take away the loaves, the fishes.
We're talking about a universal dearth,
Saharas, Gobis... desolation,
And clocks striking midnight!

Yes, Lord, I ate yesterday,
But it is passed
And there is not enough...

James Howard Trott

Baskets of fragments!

NOT ENOUGH

He cried cheerfully and tearfully smiled,
His joy so great that sorrow mild
Was pressed in service to supplement
The inadequate expression of his heart's content.

THE CRY OF THE DEAF

The paralyzed limb quivers with memory of movement and
    usage.
The blind orb turns this way and that, the missing limb itches.
There is no happy purpose, no harmony of reflex and reason
In the fluttering of the broken bird or dried leaf this season.

The deaf cry -- vocal chords respond beyond any understanding
To joy or pain or desire to communicate in strange manner
Completely incomprehensible (at least to those born unhearing):
Cry nonetheless, in peculiar grunt or high-pitched moan.

All exercise nerveless limbs, organs unfeeling, without
    experience:
Stare in the dark, sense what sense says we can't, and try
To communicate in ways we have not learned, nor can be taught,
And have no feedback for, no record of, but this unhearing cry.

Contingency, Poems 1989-2001

NO JUDAS

If there isn't a Judas in your life,
You sleep OK at night.
If there aren't any sneaks or traitors
The chances are slight
That you'll find you shared purse empty
Or that great ironic twist,
That he'll lead a crowd to kill the pal
He embraces with a kiss.
No regular deadbeat in your gang
Always sure to drop the ball?
Knacky to whimper at the bang
When he makes you fail or fall?
Well, rejecting the Judases
In many ways frees us --
But with nary a Judas in your life,
You aren't a lot like Jesus.

DEGRADATION LOOKING GOOD

Few if any of us refuse to know that scorn may be borne,
May be transmitted by air by less than a glare, by a look,
And even perchance, by a glance.

Where as children almost from the carriage, we disparaged
In open, intemperate epithet and tone, we have so grown,
That now our bile, often wears a smile.

The essence of insult is dehumanization, degradation
Of other full and worthy human beings to things,
Bidding them die by annihilating eye.

James Howard Trott

The eye is not a mere organ of sense. Its propensity
To perceive is but one of its tasks. It sends and asks,
Touches and recoils, agrees, foils.

Although modesty is a lost virtue, now rumored to hurt,
Its maxim that eyes touch, said much, much more
Than optometry's lore knows or admits.

If eyes touch, then a glance may be a blow. We know
This a convention, but there is little mention made
As such, not much, of another kind of touch.

None of us want to be things despised, but prized?
We recognize and resist a look that rejects as it inspects,
But learn we must to mistrust lust.

And even when lust's objects have learned to spurn it;
That it degrades, treats beating heart like meat mart,
Those whose eyes burn are slow to learn.

For eyes do more than see, touch and send, they reflect,
And send back the dot and dash, the soul unshuttering flash,
What they first sent begin to believe, now receive.

So the man turning the outrageous, angel-of-light pages
Of the pornographic book, like a welder at a mirror,
Blinds his own eyes with the sear flame.

His gaze lights no paper, but like the bolder raper
Of a woman, made for him un-person, he may be sure
Something is consumed, fades to ash in the hot flash.

The eyes are soul gates, both release and let in,
Sin comes and goes, ebbs and flows, washes the shores
Both outer and inner, erodes the sinner.

Degradation is not a one-way transaction, the active faction,
Whether desiring or hating, is thus always driving itself
Toward the soul-dead state it would make the other's fate.

Contingency, Poems 1989-2001

MISSED KISS

Fame, the world-renowned Gloria, I once thought to kiss.
I stood in line, I reasoned -- no not reasoning, but remiss
Of duty, of love, and of calling,
Not in desire for rising, but desire for falling.
She kissed the others there, arranged before me --
        Kin who knew her better:
For them obliging, but free.
        I sought to forge a fetter.
But though she these without demand,
When she came to me, she offered her hand.
Humiliated, I kissed but shame.
Her best of kisses was to deny my claim.

THE SENSITIVE FERN

    How often in the woods'
    One is startled
    By that one officious frond,
    That prophetic branch of fern
    Which stands up above the rest
    And flutters warnings,
    As all the rest droop calmly.
    This extreme sensitivity
    To the slightest breeze is tiresome --
    And we do not like
    Being startled.

James Howard Trott

MEMORY FADES

My memories fade,
No -- fade not they,
It is my memory fades away.
Each memory remains distinct,
Each word or breath
Each dear eye's blink.

Each ring of every chime
My clock
Distinguished. Of beloved talk
Each word or phrase
Is whole and round --
So every sight
And every sound
In this flat world
Reverberates
Within its final states.

Refers,
Yes, refers, as well
As being what
But itself can tell.
And though my mind
And memory twist --
I do not see or know or wist
All is indeed as it is indeed.

One day no memory I will need.

Contingency, Poems 1989-2001

DENYING AN INFERNO FUEL

Without refuge on the sea of plains
They watched the grassfire up the range --
Eat up the range, race and devour
Every stem and every flower --
And they were caught before it.

Caught before it they wildly turned
And looked for shelter which would not be burned --
Which would not be burned, could be reached in a hurry,
But there was nothing to withstand that fury --
They had but minutes left.

With but minutes left before things turned tragic,
One reached in his pocket for what seemed magic --
A pack of matches which he quickly struck
In an effort to beat fate or cheat bad luck
By burning the spot upon which they stood.

Burning the spot upon which they stood
They coaxed the small fire as far as they could
Until they'd a fifty yard circle of black
By the time the prairie fire hit with a crack
And they huddled before its onslaught.

They huddled before its onslaught and prayed
As sparks fell angry that the harvest was hayed,
And brown bitter smoke roiled over and on
Then suddenly cleared as the fire was gone,
Raging on, leaving them safe.

They burned their patch, the small comfort they had
Though it was not destructive, no idol, nor bad --
But by losing all, they escaped a cruel
Fate -- he who does likewise will be no fuel.

James Howard Trott

LIVING LARGE

Living large is no blessing,
Full of doubt and fear and guessing,
Every trial and every rigor --
Who, as He, would live life bigger?

MARGARET

She grew lighter the last years,
Always small, then less and less feisty.
"I'm getting married to a cop," she said --
She wasn't asking our advice or consent.
It was always news, newly tendered,
Every week, every day, new splendored --
Her wedding day with her cosmic cop
All her hope, which nothing could stop.
His descent to arrest her shrinking decline
Put spring in her step, made his badge shine.
What made the aides chuckle, friends sigh,
Seemed to put more sparkle in her eye,
Until her cop came his bride to take
-- I expect a piece of wedding cake.

SPRING FERNS

It is no wonder the animists
Stand so ready to embrace the news;
Nor is it a marvel a debased fait
Turns so quickly transcendental --

There are so many pregnant silences
In the spring woods:
Awesome pauses into which
Spirit alone can speak.
I heard them say,
Saw, tasted them --
None of these but more today
In the Jacob-laddered urns
Of lady ferns, airless spaces
Long and longing filled.

LIKE RAINDROPS

Like raindrops running down a thin tarp
So these meander, the notes of my harp.
They coagulate and hurry ever straighter together,
Thicker or thinner, depending on the weather,
And at the edge, leap, fall, in paths none can compute
Either blown spray, or water for some dry root.

A DRAMATIC PRODUCTION
(A poem written years before the movie *The Prestige*)

In this play I saw (it was a mind's eye dream) the stage
Was not wide, but a constant stream
      of actors gestured and talked
As from left to right they danced, and crawled and walked.

The orchestra sometimes chose one, then another, to accompany,
As some supported their actor brother,
    or sister, then shifted
As the director honored, the audience applauded each as gifted.

The hall hummed with anticipation, excitement, a strong sense
Of potential great enlightenment,
    of meaning significance about to emerge
From cryptic monologue and dialogue in theatrical surge.

Each grew in confidence, standing, in our estimation. They went
Across the stage, until, nearly spent,
    their progress ended in ovation
As each bowed deeply to acknowledge well-earned affirmation.

But, somewhat disturbing, (perhaps something I ate)
I imagined or was sensate to,
    at each exit, a sharp cry of terror,
Muffled by the magnificent play (perhaps I was in error).

LETTER TO EDWARD AND EMILY

    I have always respected, been taught
    To speak kindly of kindred, even those not
    Entirely sane, completely composed,
    But you test the limits, heaven knows.
    You seemed nearly oblivious to the Great God Fame,
    Offered next to nothing, hardly knew his name.
    Whom the gods would destroy they first make mad.
    Who the gods would destroy first eradicates desire,
    Or directs it not to fellow man or self or to minor Pan,
    But to a God much higher.

Contingency, Poems 1989-2001

EAVESDROPPING ON ANGELS

To hear about hell beaten backwards, great antiphonies ring
Over one soul once in bondage, now suddenly set a-wing
Is a divine sort of caddishness, almost like eavesdropping,
A psycho-logical addiction which knows no stopping.

To hear about the flesh put to rout, about new hearts saying no
To things they never thought they could ever answer so;
To see faces and lives transformed by graces beyond conceiving,
Hear echoed from dear, deepening depths, bounding bells of
      believing.

Yes, we were present there (there perhaps or in glory).
Spoke perhaps one excited word (as a child during a story).
But the power of Jesus Christ performed as we acted (as props)
And listened in awe to angel accounts like one who eavesdrops.

LEARNING CURVE

When they say there is a kind of graph,
I listen, and you know, I laugh --
For as I've very little earned,
I next to nothing ever learned.
Yet those few things I've learned to date,
I will admit, I've not learned straight.

James Howard Trott

ARE YOU THE MAN?
(Good Friday, 1993)

I asked him to be sure what I returned was rightly
His or his agency to demand -- the man at the station
Who asked first if what the defective machine rendered
Was thus and so as expected and advertised.

"Are you the man?" I said, before handing him
The extra coins of change. It wasn't quite the same
As asking if he were King of the Jews, since
I was really only one of the faceless, loud crowd.

It did not strike me until later
'Twas on Good Friday, I was enroute,
When my question was answered by another
Representative of Caesar first, "Ecce Homo".

Then I thought, the man -- as I meant it
But also perhaps unknowing, as Pilate did --
The man, the representative not only of authority,
But perhaps the only one appropriate, the epitome.

He had been shaken, as I, we were, by the disorder,
The malfunctioning of the machine, the universe,
In Jesus' answers -- they didn't add up right,
Hinted at obscure and numinous Roman superstitions.

The talk of truth he dismissed -- philosophy was Greek;
But the possibility of a son of a god
Could only be quelled by the timely Jewish reminder --
To acknowledge another king but Caesar wouldn't do.

Yet this prisoner's grasp of the derivative nature
Of authority -- always coming from above
Struck chords against which the mob's cries
Of "Barrabas" and "Crucify" clashed clangorously.

"The man" at the station was indeed ready to show tokens
When I asked to be sure of his authority,
But he did not in the slightest defer the decision
To me. He as much as said of himself, "ecce homo".

LEAPFROG

The metaphor is in my way,
I cannot hear the story . . .

The creature stands athwart my path
It blocks its maker's glory . . .

A brother blocks my high horizon
I cannot find my way . . .

Unless I put my thin hands out and on,
And leap across, not about, each
To the place of progress
Prepared for me
After another
Stays his hands on me.
I hop, they leap, we travel beyond;
By means of others go up, go on.

James Howard Trott

EMPTY-HANDED AGAIN

He grabbed my purse, my brief, my wallet, my portfolio, my
  manuscript,
He took my music, my instrument, all with which I was
  equipped,
My diary, my journals, my accounts, my records, and my graphs
Even his rewards, his gifts, tokens earned on his behalf.

With these I was pledged to serve him, nothing withheld or
  withdrawn,
Until he snatched them from me, like a king who takes his own
  pawn.
Even as first I was I am: empty-handed, no use at all.
His ways are beyond me,(seldom seem sane) I await the whim of
  his call.

Suddenly from the dark, he delivers so much, I but gasp:
Supplies, tools for new service, plans,... other hands to grasp.
As bare ground most tillable, emptied hands are most fillable.

FAITH QUESTIONS

None submits who does not question --
Indeed, demands like Job.
Had Adam and Eve asked for answers
Perhaps we'd remain disrobed.
Moses was curious to know God's name,
Asked to speak with the Judge.
Elijah wanted a conference with God,
Until he heard, wouldn't budge.
Faith questions like a lady:
Therefore one, its epitome,
Mary, simply believing, asked
"How can these things be?"

Contingency, Poems 1989-2001

IT'S SCARY TO WATCH PEOPLE MARRY

It's scary to watch people marry.
Not all the tears are pure sorrow or pure joy,
There's also fear, for two so dear,
There is something terrible in their open eagerness,
The fully candid, unsophisticated whole-hearted
Giving of themselves to one another.
Oh brother! It gives me chills!
There's not enough of reservation,
No "plan B"s, no security clause,
It makes me pause -- what of self-preservation!
It's scary to watch people marry!

FOR RICHER OR FOR POORER

Let the brother of low degree rejoice in that he is exalted:
But the rich, in that he is made low: ... James 1:9-10

> Owe no man anything, but...and yet, what are these
> Vows if not IOUs set loose on him/her who agrees.
> There are no longer any distinctions, categorical
> Divisions, except for a few metaphorical ones,
> Not even male and female, as both recite
> This formula, somewhat more than rite.
>
> Richer or poorer in time, down the line,
> But also wealth and poverty now. The vow
> Refers to what she has and lacks,
> His droughts and cataracts as they stand.
> The surfeits, famines unplanned will out
> In God's good time they know little about.

They receive each other despite blight in bud,
Regardless of where apparent deserts will flood,
Receive, take wholeheartedly without reservation,
In abandon, disavowing cordial hesitation at last,
As the Groom did, so now the Bride
In all her members; do so they beside.

IS GOD

Is God fickle
Said the straw to the sickle.

Is God just
Said the iron to the rust.

Is God love
To the hawk said the dove.

Is God good,
Said Robin Hood.

NOT SPELLS BUT PRAYERS

Spoke against the powers of dark that threaten
Us with more than imagined hells and fretting;
Cried against obscure sparks that deceive us
And other mumbled, scribbled spells more grievous:
We need words as true as honest -- enduring
Up the ages' changing stairs through obscuring

Webs of fashion clinging to us at each floor.
We reach a lighted attic by prayer -- no more.
They who whistle in the lightless places their own
Tunes to words ostentatious, putting trust
In no revelation but their own tongues' trips are shown
Not even themselves -- lose at last their grips and moan.
But if we listen, discern before speak
Not spells but prayers we learn from whom we seek.

THE INDEPENDENT SCRIBE

The independent scribe is a rarity --
Scribes are usually found with the Pharisee.

NAKEDNESS IS NOT JUST SKIN DEEP
(After my last check-up)

Nudes are said to be beautiful,
But the naked are helpless.
So before the lady doctor I was forced to revise
What I am and appear in my own and others eyes.
I was no nude, but susceptible flesh.
We wear attractive clothes if we are dutiful
To armor ourselves against too close assessment.
Since flesh itself may tremble
We fashionably dissemble
And calculate what others' dress meant.

James Howard Trott

We would be best dressed like Arab ladies,
Veiled fully against the dangerous rush
Which wells from deep heart places,
Proclaims deeper than our skin, we blush.

IF CRIME IS NATURAL

If the criminal does what he does,
Only naturally as he must,
Then of course we have no right to condemn
Or live in fear, disapproval, mistrust.

The worms at your grandmother's funeral
Can't be condemned for their taste,
Though few of us feel we're suffiently kin
For welcome or warm embrace.

GRACE IS FOUND IN LOW PLACES

    The air is thin on the mountain.
    Its waters run downhill.
    Winter drives all life to the valley.
    We meet on our knees -- and still.

Contingency, Poems 1989-2001

THE HARP OF GOD'S GUTS

If you find it hard to believe God in flesh
Wept over the world
And his favorite city with pity,
If you can not analogize without a type
Think it pure hype to say He loves,
Then this my challenge:
Listen an hour to the wind.
I find it infallibly changes my warp,
The harp of God's guts weeps a sad tune,
The flute of his sorrow
Whimpers over our sin,
Listen. Again.

SLIDING SCALE OF SIGNIFICANCE

Gold to the starving is much the same
As if it were lead or dung.
New widows hear every song a dirge,
No matter how well sung.
To the plush and pampered a fly in the pot
May make a tempest of tea.
While pain is humdrum to those grown numb
Through lifelong misery.

So beware my friend when your teachings tend
To prescribe before you know
What your hearers suffer: whether mild or rougher
Winds those frail barks blow.
For we constantly learn that we can't discern
Wisdom apart from the man's
Who has slid the length, to weakness from strength
On the scale of significance.

James Howard Trott

HAP HAZARD

It happens that I might...
Hap' I should happen on it...
What happened was a mishap,
'Twas a matter of happenstance.
Mayhap he will,
Perhaps she won't.
Happily we may...
It was a happy day...
Aren't you happy that...
He made them happy by...
I'm happy she's happy,
Is everybody happy?

Is there really such a thing
As the pursuit of happiness?
Or perhaps hap-piness
Is the pursuer.

GRAVING IMAGES

The gnawing incisive teeth of sin are graving images for me
    again --
Graving images for me and of me to insure that I and others love
    me.

In pagan display parading potential or religious ritual, evidential
Piety and purity: beautiful bosh -- I write my graffiti, slop
    hogwash.

Not even thought murders or adulteries are as dear to our hearts
    as these

Scurrilous sculptures in clay and wood: imaged beauty, power, good.

Demons aren't transfixed in casts nor gods incarnate in plated plasts.
It is ourselves we bow before; my own image I make and adore.

This heart-molding instinctive gnaw, hastens us to the grave's craw:
To a graven stone and a smoking chasm -- or an Image wreaking iconoclasm.

GUERILLAS GOING IN

Guerillas going in extend themselves in turn --
Through doors, to corners, crouch and hide
And hold their weapons at the ready.

Any foe, resistance found, they face and fight,
By ones and twos and one by one
Nor halt and faint, for fallen friend.

This is no hopscotch game of joy,
Delight nor gain in exercise;
Nor concept built of heaping words.

Deadly is the game they play.
Fearful is each forward spin.
Naught but love and hatred's goal
Could keep guerilla's going in.

James Howard Trott

ONCE SEVEN
(After seeing my father's siblings)

Once seven, concentrated, so to speak,
Like summer concentrated in a wine.
Gone are three, so gone the seven;
Gone the four, too, though somewhere.
Once one, now fewer -- many,
Out across rivers, roads, beliefs.
Once seven, concentrated, so to speak,
Like joy concentrated in a song.
Still are three, but really still seven;
Still four, really, though every where.
Once one, now fewer, many; still one,
Out across rivers, roads, beliefs.
Still one -- more one, though multiplied.
One as seven were one, more -- expanded --
One as hundreds are.
As seven were one, all once were one.

THE GLORY OF THE LAUREL

Though I walk amidst the laurel,
It's beauty is not mine --
So profuse and fine its coral,
No rival claims a quarrel.
Yet a sorrow here I find
As I stand amidst the laurel --
That it's glory is not mine.

Contingency, Poems 1989-2001

HEROD AND JUDAS

Whether we are bent at all costs on preventing
The usurping of our throne
Or precipitately pursuing the culmination
Of this vision of our own
Makes little difference, friend or foe:
There's but one to whom or from whom we can go.
We can resist him, kill his cohort
In space and time,
Attempt to influence him
By main force, by reason or rhyme,
But in the end there are few choices,
No matter what we try:
To die with him and for him --
Or just to die.

GOD'S BARE BODY

God's little body came along as we: naked and helpless,
Strangely free of his mother's close womb, forced, the air
To breathe cold, sharp; and barely born, was again wrapped,
This time in man-made clothes, as tight perhaps as any
Human clothes would ever be, restraining his limbs,
Which bare of flesh and free of cloth wore stars and wind.

God's naked name, high tetra-grammaton, brushed flesh early,
Adam's tongue stammered on blissfully, naming creatures,
Yes, but also spoke with God, speech sure and innocent,
He thought nothing odd in dialogue with his Creator,
Nor need to dress --. It was later his wife, wishing to sup,
(She his first song of praise) taught him to dress up.

James Howard Trott

Then Noah outlandishly decked out in a wave-washed ark
Embodied God's will, just a spark of the anointing, carried
It and other leaven, disappointing, but was made efficient,
Told and showed animal hides could not adequately adorn,
But meat be eaten and sacrificed down to Abraham, the founder,
Who like most in God's garments was both saint and bounder.

Joseph exceptionally, dressed in gift of exuberance,
Never gave hubris a chance on other occasions, suffered long
Through no fault of his own, frequently found faithful
Despite trying circumstances as when he took full flight,
From his master's wife who would have him to bed,
His innocence made him guilty; it was naked he fled.

Jesus hung naked -- again -- Od's bodkin! How much guff,
Much humility is enough! Crucified on a tree he watched,
Like a million times before, as they cast lots for his garments --
The centurion kept the score. Clothed there, not with flesh,
Not with rasping cloth -- it was an eternity of hells he doffed --
And wore them out so thoroughly, the next day put them off.

There were other naked fears and flights then, as now --
One young man at Christ's arrest, like Joseph fled (not how),
And when the last day comes it will be a sorry varmint,
Who makes the mistake of going back for his garment.

Now God's garment, put off so many little ways, 'til at last,
He put off nearly everything, has passed in mystic pawn-
    exchange
So we whose clothes Christ wore, strangely are clothed again
In the righteousness, glory; sufficient now, never to hide,
At the expiration of pride, we'll see his face unveiled nigh.

Feeling still a bit bare, we long to be fully clothed on high
    -- with bodies like his.

Contingency, Poems 1989-2001

THE TWO ORGANS OF SEX

Propriety will be offended by this modest explanation,
By the absence of titillation and voyeur's fodder.
But I am brazen, and odd and unembarrassedly find
The two organs of sex are the skin and the mind.

The skin and the mind, the mind and the skin,
Two organs of love, two organs of sin.
Their juxtaposition may lead to a state
Of ecstasy, misery, love, or hate.

When either skin or mind try to fly solo,
(or two skins or two minds attempt meiosis),
The transaction is doomed to be completely hollow,
Accruing more longing than of it disposes.

Some synaptic connection between mind and skin
Makes each integral both to the other:
As everyone had both father and mother;
So every act both these participate in.

The fact that their trial marriages so often sour
May indicate mind and skin need more permanent rites
Than ecstatic liaisons of but half an hour
Before thin-skinned days and troubled-minded nights.

Mind and skin are the organs of sex, but sex is an organ, too
In a larger organism, man, the creature me and you.
As mind needs skin (and skin, mind) so sex needs soul.
So man needs the Spirit of God to know himself whole.

James Howard Trott

FOR HEAVEN'S SAKE

'For Heaven's sake, son!'
With a certain irony
Of exasperation in the voice:
An ego-deflating,
An undercutting,
A denial of worth.

And sometimes it was right,
But, oh, too often
It was wrong --
Only the self-defending
Frustration of an adult
Who felt his own failure
And didn't know whose
Sake he said it for.

HIGH GULL

I saw him high awash
On the wrack of wind-torn skies,
Gulling me to follow him until
At last, lost in the ruin of his will,
He entered the knowledge of things unseen.
His wings frail-feathered grasped out
Toward reaches which pulled him on,
As though he longed to lose himself; and did,
Like men who seek by any means
To drop, lose hold that vestige, they,
Yet know not what they do.
Do Satan-seekers know Satan?
Or seekers of self-annihilation?
Unless, at last, indeed they know,
At the moment they are gone.

That gull, gull no longer to me,
   Did not let go, but sheered firm-willed,
   Knew his desire and to what he flew,
   Having sailed and spoke the heights before.

FIRST CLUES

Staying with a cousin young days on the farm,
I learned with a shock that chickens indeed do
Run around with their heads cut off.
I also learned that life included chores,
And chores pain.
His daily task was to feed
Those birds with the superfluous heads,
And carry two bucketfuls of water
From the heavy iron pump across to the coop,
So I set out to carry one.
The bail cut terribly into my hand.
Based on observations, I began to suspect
Something had gone wrong with the universe.

THINGS BURIED

Bury hatchets, bury swords -- and they will rust,
And come to nothing, nothing but dust.
Bury a seed -- a soldier's joke --
And you're likely to get a pine or oak
      --In time.

James Howard Trott

Power is measured in these two manners:
By the glint of the sword and those hidden banners,
Tiny leaves marking a small seed's demise --
One day to tower through dusk-rust skies
    --One day.

Illusions of power still cut and kill --
But superman's strength dies with his will.
Eternal things, true things of might
Spring from sparks buried by night
    --Soon.

FIREFLY CODE

The fireflies flick their trail of tales
Across the woods and fading sky.
Their semiotics is obscure
In codes and calls meant for eye
Or eyes compounded for their race
Of luciferin and luciferinase.
Each species has its own tattoo:
'Darling, I'm in love with you.'
But others send out disinformous light,
Mimicking sensual species quite
Clearly so that suitors who sweeten
To the call may well be eaten.
At last decoded, all the dashings of men
So dimly distinct, but these two signs send.

Contingency, Poems 1989-2001

HONOR AMONG THIEVES

Why do we love Robin Hood so dearly, when clearly his sort
Are few. Few and far between at best, this Rorschach test
Shows something of our psyches. Robinhood-like we all
    imagine
Ourselves honorable thieves, driven but pure, wounded
    without ordure.

But he who knows thieves nothing believes of the pretty myth:
Not policemen, judges or jailers, nor parole officers or bailers,
Nor other thieves, nor thief mothers, nor cousins, uncles,
    brothers.
There is only small honor for a brief time among those in crime.

And where this small honor exists, its essence consists in
Mutual fear or persuasion, equal incapacity for evasion,
In various kinds of stalemates among various kinds of jailmates:
In the knowledge "I could hurt you," not some heart-born
    virtue.

Few thieves there are with motives to make votives of the pure.
(Nor are there many pure to be sure to be votives.) Who
    believes
In anything honorable or high for which any live or die?
There's no honor at all among, and but once hung between
    thieves.

FIRE-BUILDING

No fool our enemy, he knows the best fire
Is not tyrant's holocaust, nor martyr's pyre.
He loves not the sacrifice soaked with faith or love,
Susceptible to no flames but those from above.
His best delight is a properly crackling blaze
Fueled by living limbs, hearts and days,

James Howard Trott

A fire on his own hearth -- he likes nothing more.
He knows the boy scout tricks with which to make it roar.
No fool our enemy, he starts by learning
Which of the logs dragged from the burning
May be covered from the daily dew and weather
To be slowly seasoned until ready to burn together,
Until each the renewed flames is unable to hinder --
Until each has gathered to him his own pile of tinder.

IMAGES OF CHRIST

It is not hard to see the poor as Christ --
Not hard in the head, because he said
That as we did kind things to this one and that
We did so unto him (or did not do!)
But the rich or kings or elder brothers
In our place and time seem wholly other
From Him, despite the fact he's called as much
And seems to call us to recognize that, too.

FALL FISH

The fish are dying . . .
The trout belly brooks many a spot,
The salmon scales fall,
They dart, they weave
Singly and in shoals.

Contingency, Poems 1989-2001

They scatter in sparks of dying
Like embers into ashes
Before a shark
Like the wind.

But fewer and fewer
Lurk still in accustomed holes
Behind the branch barren
That sustained them.

Most float ashore
But some die iridescent
Still sailing on the water. See
One floats there brilliant belly up.

It flashes against the gray
And obscure of the autumn stream,
Dim and opalescent with
The flowing away of the year.

NIGHT'S LADY

Dark eyes open on a desert night,
(Desert without flowers, night without stars)
Standing on the corner by a city bar,
Dancing slowly to the drum of delight.

Delight in the ears, delight for men,
But desperate hunger for a stallion to ride:
A shot in the arm, a dim room rite.
In a trick or two catch the horse again.

The horse she desires, the deep desert scenes,
The mount to bear her through concrete ravines

Are not forthcoming -- for other mounts come,
Four horses hooves to a different drum...

Unless through the dark of her active despair
She catches the knight who rescues the fair.

FAINT DISAPPROVAL

Faint disapproval would not be so faint
If it were a virtue becoming a saint.
Disapproving faintly is a dim reflex,
A dignified version of the impulse to hex.
Faint disapproval never good conscience moved,
Should be by good conscience much disapproved.

IT'S WRONG TO DIE FOR THE DEAD

Sacrifice may not be at its popular height these days,
But most admit at weak moments it pays to give, to offer, to
 spend
For the good of another, a kinsman, a friend.

Parents, missionaries, a loyal employee or two
Give without ado much of their lives for others good, success,
Often without any expectation of reward or redress.

Soldiers in battle, firefighters and police
Literally give lives to where they cease, and laurels crown
 graves,
For the supreme actor is the dead who a living saves.

Contingency, Poems 1989-2001

Only a small twist, however, and the glory dims:
None prizes or praises, sings hymns to who dies for the dead,
Rather recoils in horror and pity instead.

The wives in old India, the suttee suicides,
Were no heroines; nor does proper pride accrue to who seeks to avenge
A dead kinsman in sacrificial revenge.

Old causes, lost traditions, empty names and houses --
Although the dreamer such espouses aren't objects for self abnegation.
Not even the cross worth sacrifice, were it the last station.

EXUBERANCE AND ENTHUSIASM

When Adriel was born I could not help
My shouting, my jumping,
My acting like a fool --
All unconscious.

As lunacy is to the moon
(A sports fan to a game)
So enthusiasm is to God,
And all his mighty works --
God in one.

Exuberance, however,
Owes its derivation
To the idea of great fertility,
An abundance of flower and fruit.

James Howard Trott

When Adriel was born,
I suppose I acted like a fool
Out of both enthusiasm and
A sense of exuberance.

And may it be true again, oh Lord
At your return.

JAWBONE OF AN ASS

Of all the weapons employed by Bible warriors, none
Is so singularly apropos our times as this peculiar one,
With which Samson slew so many Philistines,
And with which Joab defended kings and queens.
Even more amazingly, one was used to stop Balaam.
Imitation prophet's beasts still know how to regale 'em.
We have so divorced talk and life we've come to the passes
Where Christians fall steadily 'neath jawbones of asses.

EMPTY PACKAGE

What drives us like madmen, what's it all about?
Why open up the package when love is left out?
Why think about the wrapping, why touch the bows?
When the inside's dark and hollow, each of us knows?

We know the present's empty, because the first time
Someone gave it to us, it was loveless as a crime.
Yet some fool thing in us keeps up the delusion,
And we go seeking more, compelled, in confusion.

Contingency, Poems 1989-2001

Why think about the gown, when there is no bride?
Why open up a package with nothing inside?

It's the something left out we seek, again, again,
To accumulate nothings enough to pretend,
There was once something, will be something soon
A mystery, a riddle, a rite, a rune.

Nothing
In the package
Don't whimper, don't pout --
Why open up the package when love is left out?

EXPLORER

My lover's face,
A mountain range, lies still
Nor could I make
Too much of the smallest mole-hill.
Each new-lit crag
Each solemn slope
Echoes grandeur
From the last.
And subtle roseate atmospheres
Proclaim the whole more vast
Than this discoverer
From high morning though he gaze
Could ever explore adequately
Had he as many more days.

LAOCOON

He spoke truth, saw deeply into the hearts and gifts of the
    Greeks
Was priest in the midst of holy rite, one who Olympus seeks,
But the blood of his bull was not enough; no not even his own;
Nor could the blood of his sons suffice to deliver or atone.
The serpents got him, then the gods forgot him.

WASHED WAYWARD FEET

Jesus washed wayward feet, knowing full well,
That while he was burning hell up in himself,
They would be tiptoe fled, denying --
Swearing agnosticism certain as cock crying.

He loved away their dirt knowing the muck
They'd soon truck in over the floor;
The fungus, sin, between the toes flowering
That never goes away despite much scouring.

Towel girt, he called for leaders like slaves,
Not waited on hand and foot, but waiting;
And humiliating beyond rational conceiving,
He loved them, all traitors and deceiving.

Contingency, Poems 1989-2001

ELI SAT

Eli sitting on his seat
By the doorposts of the Temple of the Lord
Thought Hannah drunk
For her silent prayers
That her honor be restored.

Then she explained not wine
But sorrow filled her strange tears there,
And Eli told her, Go in peace,
The Lord will grant your prayer.

Hannah had the son she longed for --
More than wine or meat,
While Eli toppled over one day
Too fat for his seat.

RULES OF PRECEDENCE

Lady Macbeth, all things gone chaotic,
Abandoned fond hopes at the crowning dinner.
Her husband, bloody-handed king, was obsessed,
With the ruin his hag-ridden vision and acts
Had brought and bolstered with more blood yet.
Therefore, giving up her comfortable feast,
She bade knights and ladies in whom fear was growing,
Not stand upon the order of their going.

Take not the highest seat, our Lord warned,
Lest another come in and your host put you down.
Take the lowest seat, and receive greater honor,
When the lord of the banquet bids you ascend.

James Howard Trott

Both Lady Macbeth and the come-down Son,
Spoke against a backdrop of ancient manners --
In which eldest, wisest, highest in rank
Went first: making exception from precedence.

On entering a room, in sitting at table,
While introducing members of family or guests,
The greatest goes first, most highly honored.

God the oldest, wisest, strongest,
Built and entered universal room
First of all, and bade others follow:
Powers, principalities, archangels, angels,
Men, animals, plants and minerals.

And we, insofar as we consent to courtesy,
Confess our sins, first to him, the Highest.
Then forgive each other, for precedence never
Allows charity but one focus and object.
The Macbeths made that error -- mesmerized
With the highest position, thinking it all.
So much they revered it, that they despised it,
As we killed God to usurp his throne.

But He had consented already to death,
Had taken the low seat, low unto hell,
And gave us his life, that none could take,
In order that we might move in a dance --
Swiftly down from the high seat we wrested,
Then back to a higher from our humbled-heart least.
Wherefore now precedence continues fluid,
And the proud immobile alone are thought rude.

Contingency, Poems 1989-2001

EARLY CONTENDER

I awake every morning, coward of life,
Rung to the ring for another bloody round.
Huddled in my bed afraid to leave my corner
Until my trainer pushes me stumbling
Toward the fears the bells sound.

There is no opponent, just a motley tag-team
Who do not embody, are not my dread.
Fear, itself and my own cowardice
Are the defending champions --
I'd fight anyone instead.

Temptation, mortality, pain and angst
Have each already scheduled a bout.
I can hardly believe my hero,
The All-time Reigning Champion,
Got up each morning and went out.

MOWING THE NEIGHBOR'S LAWN

It was a cause of considerable heat, drove my father to distraction,
And drives me there now, too, in the same ageless reaction,
When a son spends a morning mowing a neighbor's yard
Despite weeks of regretting his own jobs as much too hard.

Not just lawns -- but raking leaves and hauling trash or wood,
Seem to be recreational everywhere in the neighborhood,
Except on one's own turf, in one's own territory,
Where they're terrible tasks and tortures: a much different story.

James Howard Trott

Why are others' tasks much easier than duties of our own?
I'll admit it of a great many things and not only for boys alone.
Perhaps it's a rule of the universe, dating back to the world's
    dawn --
Even God's son couldn't resist taking care of his neighbor's lawn.

UNTIL I AM DISTRAUGHT

I will presume upon your grace, if you do not treat
Me severely enough, Lord, as a captive in your train.
I will play the Pharisee, the sycophant, for gain,
While my heart sends another psalm in every beat
To earless, eyeless idols who never find me out.
They can not tell my service the dullest dubious sort,
They know not whisper's or sidelong glance's import.
They cannot pull me up, stop me or turn me about.
Their companions crackle in the flames, no more forlorn,
No less prone to perception, no more capable of care
For mortal so far astray, so thorough iniquity-borne.
They have not, can not enter in as you have, to share
This despair. Nearly destroy me, if all else availeth not,
Distress, distrain me Lord until I am distraught.

COST ACCOUNTING

An obscure Nazarene invented economics
Referring to a universal audit which would lay all books bare.
He spoke of barn and tower builders,
Religious profiteers, and especially the poor

(He had a penchant for the poor) --
Those hopeless talliers of pennies and nothing.

Which of you does not count the cost, he said,
Count the cost, count the cost -- of what?
Of farm and ecclesiastical buildings?
Of nothing?

Text book examples were well-known in his day:
Job invested wisely and where did it get him?
Jonah counted accurately and knew where his interests lay.
Who was this Jesus to wrap it all up so succinctly?

But this accounting professor unlike most others
Went into the marketplace, planned his venture,
A real arbitrageur, sweating denarius drops of blood
Upon the floor of the garden as the terms were fixed --
And paid.

CROSSING THE RED SEA

To hurry -- that was the thing gripped us all
After the first shock.
We cried out in awe and fear, at first,
But at his urging plunged down --
There was really no choice --
Egypt's chariots raised dust behind us
All across the plain.
So we hurried.
And I hurry still,
Staring at the mountainous walls of water
Poised there, teeming, boiling,
Thick with destruction -- seeming
Perhaps to begin breaking

James Howard Trott

Back into their rightful channels.
I hurry -- and forget who
Parted the sea -- and why -- and for whom.

OFFERINGS AS WHISKEY

Perhaps it would be better to say small beer or dregs.
Were this the typical exhortation so we might,
But mine is a different burden, my question begs
Not over how much but to what degree we've gotten tight.

Whiskey is a distillation of fermented stuff kept stored
In charred barrels for a decade or so,
Just as the members of the church seem to hoard
Their "tithe" of what they do or know.

And let them ferment in vats from other gods
Then distill them through trial into chests and casks
Until they form the essence of ends and odds
Of their darkened hopes and side-tracked tasks.

We gather around the altar like the boys at the bar,
Where our weekly potion is poured into baskets,
Instead of glasses, but the differences are,
Insignificant as lives poured into caskets.

It's true the Lord paid some heed to tax,
And spoke about money and living,
But he never let money-changers relax.
He needs no distillers or well-aged giving.

Contingency, Poems 1989-2001

COURTS POET

The coy sylph -- not coy but fay
Who dances through imagine's glades
Comes never to the looking eye
But flits and feints and fades.

Clam'rous youth demands her presence,
Scribbles rhymes empty of essence,
Until he wills to have nor hold her --
Then she puts her hand upon his shoulder.

GOD IS NOT CAREFUL

God is not careful of my kingdom come,
(Cunningly coming just next his one) --
Not properly courteous as between lords.
He usurps my lands, my vassals, my hoards.

God is not careful of my sense of myself:
He stacks my best talents on a dusty shelf,
Won't allow me to be what I'm oft reputed,
Demands just the deeds for which I'm least suited.

God is not careful of my valuable time,
(He skews my rhythm, he wracks my rhyme)
Wastes my best hours, my days and years,
Hangs all on moments I'm disabled by tears.

God is not careful of my well-wrought plans,
My longest labors, my well-armed stands.
He sends me on errands of which I know nought,
He denies me the harvests most dearly bought.

James Howard Trott

God is not careful of my memorabilia,
Regards my lot as Hamlet, Ophelia:
Derides my scrapbook, laughs at my hobbies
As sensitively as a bar full of swabbies.

God is not careful of my painstaking cares,
He pounds my penates, leans on my lares.
He is downright careless of my life and limb,
And demands in return that I care full for Him!

CONSPICUOUS KEYS

He stands at ease, content, perhaps proud,
Although he makes no claim out loud,
He wears conspicuous and gleaming bright
His life's credentials where no one's sight
Can miss them in their intricate tangle,
Or fail to hear their comforting jangle.
His joy we envy, how often I've felt
The desire to have a lot more keys on my belt.

OLD STUMP, NEW TREE

Withered in the heat of brown-bark fire,
Its contorted sinewy talons clutching in death,
It's wings curled in trembling farewell
For flight from smoke and crumbling ash nest,
The old stump gives birth a phoenix.

Contingency, Poems 1989-2001

Straining forth from the matter in which it's bound
The volcanic cone rises to a peak,
Dark and sterile in it's longing forth,
Its mute gathering force to speak
A fiery volley of flowing life.

Wrapped in the bindings of its spun shroud
The carcase lies still, but an outlined bundle:
No wings, no limbs, no features, to reveal,
What was this creature now its captor's meal:
An arachnid towering over its nurturing victim.

A corpus of research, an historical compendium,
The brown-bound, mildew-scented library heap
Registers no surprise, no envy, no scolding
Seems to slumber the old scholar's sleep;
While a clumsy disciple cobbles out his dissertation.

The black birches in these woods
More often than not, grow out of old stumps --
(Birch stumps or not, I don't know, but doubt.)
There's something spectral in their familiarity:
Some tradition or rite we've forgotten about.

COMES AROUND

Hindu doctrines of karmic carousel impose a flux
On both heaven and hell -- No ultimate beginning or end --
Each transgression against the cosmic code carries its load
Of buckshot baggage, weighs each soul with a gravity
Inescapable, a toll takes, that soul remakes
In form of creature low (a flea) or higher (a cow).

James Howard Trott

Old Norse hopes of eternal reward hung on the sword,
A one-time earthly battlefield visit with perquisite gain,
Heaven's cycle -- being slain, slaying, in valorous Valhalla,
In the glory, not squalor of battle, not cattle or beasts;
Glory days vary slightly, the gore ending nightly
With the slain resurrected for tales, drink, and feasts.

Those doctrines may be said to be ancient, but the patient
Student of the present times will find strangely true,
As saying and cue, for much of what men do -- what
Goes out, returns, whether bread on the water, or mythological
Image of joy -- the sacred cow becomes the spotted owl,
And Valhalla the corner bar where heroes hoot and howl.

We think our philosophy of fate sterner, nothing spurious,
Because yesterday's dead-serious becomes today's delirious;
Yesterday's precarious, today's hilarious, and so our forebears
Receive no respect, our lares lie languishing, our puny penates--
But to my point, the current scion of fate, elected, crowned,
Has as its motif and motto "what goes . . ., comes around."

Strange doctrine, strangely true, a principle rightly handled,
That lights up some dim corners, bad eggs candled thereby
Show sooner or later as rotten, though the hen brood long,
God patiently waits, and freedom and fate seem to conspire
To give enough rope, or haywire, to the desperately clever,
It almost seems like never, before "goes" becomes "comes."

It is a doctrine that applies beyond the skies, in the same sense
The strange offense against balance and justice, which allows that
The innocent be sat in the chair of judgment to receive, not give
What equity would grudge. Sent voluntary, the Word who made,
Who holds all together, and cannot be gainsayed, took in hand
The injury, injustice; by God was damned for sinful man.

If that's what goes around coming around again, how awful
The application to men, for whom the lawful application death
Is more deserved than the current breath and taken full force

Contingency, Poems 1989-2001

As proposition logical, the fatal becomes the last theological;
God less than fate; Christ, not to the Father subordinate
But to a proposition, a saying heard on the street.

We must then, speaking in those terms of Christ's work,
Admit what comes he sends, what goes he alone releases,
We cannot philosophically pretend his death was finally just.
Just this relation between: his death was our due come askew,
Our healing -- his lack; our stripes -- his back; mercy
Turned justice. He freely took when we were brought to book.

Such cosmos-kicking disregard for fatal principle must
Have incalculable effects, on spheres, men and dusty motes,
Were gravity repealed, attraction and repulsion, no greater
Convulsion would result, no mighty mourn, no lowly exult
More fully or more freely or with more perplexity, confusion,
For such an abdication is the greatest revolution.

Yet in the divine courtesy, the old law is not erased,
Those who wish to live by tit for tat, may still run the race,
Those who think their karma will keep them may still try,
Those who wish to live by the sword, by the sword may die.

And, emptied now of utility like slide rule in age of computer,
The principle remains metaphor, a necessary refuter of another
Principle, that romantic illusion that liberty means license,
That chaos out of confusion, Christ upsetting cosmic tables,
Delivers all in midst of sin, the manure-filled Augean stables
Though still unclean, rendered fit for the god to dwell in.

What goes around, they say, will return, what built up one day
Will return: who leaves his husks and porcine companions,
Has two returns: first home -- of mercy, then servanthood --
The results of the curse he brought on himself after Adam first
Brought it on his family. Burdened by another, by another
We're freed, still cursed with our own earthly results and need.

And who goes around, ought to come around again, for we
Are told to love others as he loved his friends. Those other lost

James Howard Trott

We came out from among, deserve no more fully than we
The karma they've earned, the life of the flea, eternal hell,
Everlasting reruns, awful memorial recapitulations -- names
And faces fate worse than any kind of flames incinerate.

Go, he said, go out, go around, in widening circles, find
Where may be found, those who will receive you, who will
Receive me, and dwell with them, and teach them and free
Them from the cycles of sin and hatred and lust, and send them;
Go, too, or shake off the dust from your feet where rejected,
That, too, will come back last trumpet, thunder's last crack.

Come, he said, all you laden with weights too great, weary,
Come I am the way and the gate, lay that burden down,
Take this light one up, receive bread and wine freely, sate
Yourselves on the abundance you can't buy, then gather
The fragments, pass them on; come and die, the light cross
I give you who follow into, and out of the world I call
All who understand come and go, all who a new law would
Live and know, all who can laugh at new life in an old law,
New harmony in the old sound of what truly goes,
Truly comes around -- Centurions know come and go.

ON A NOVEL WITH MISSING PAGES

Though many of your fellows have whiled for me the hours,
Called me Watson, intrigued with extraordinary powers,
Whisked me from drab practice into moors and murders and
 mists,
Never before has one left me thus, treated me like this.

Always before I have rested secure you would nobly entertain
 me.

You would involve, inform, confuse, puzzle, constrain me --
But when all was said and done, all that was done would be
      said,
And as the detective summarized, I would nod my head.

I have trusted in these excursions, these elaborate
      peregrinations
Into other cultures and lives, stretching imagination,
To rest my mind, my soul and heart from my own deductive
      strife,
Where I seldom seem to find a clue to the mystery of life.

But here, alas, I'm left tottering on a chasm's precipice,
The plot that thickened evaporates into something less than
      mist.
The cozy insights disperse, leaves in a storm that rages:
Much I ought to know is gone -- blown away on the missing
      pages.

Ah -- Is that your clue, your subtlety. You detected my motive!
You knew my heart, my plan to escape in my reading like a
      votive.
You brought me to this denouement to reveal more than I
      thought:
To teach me 'though pages aplenty be missed, there still is a
      Plot.

CLAY AND POTTER

>The clay answers to the potter
>Only when it feels it has been
>Always a pot -- and will not
>Come to memory's heel
>Of his hand, to the wheel

Where he planned and perfected not
A vessel but clay.
When we remember that day
And our nature know,
We no longer speak so.

CHRIST AS PROJECTION

Jesus indeed is only what you'd have him be.
He doth appear no other way than as you clothe him.
He comes as your reflection:
If you see yourself of sin overwhelmed and weighed,
He comes to you become full sin, who paid.
If, however, you see yourself righteous and pure,
He comes to you holy and will not demure
To sit upon the judgment throne,
For when he comes again He will no more atone.
Receive Christ, or else know His rejection . . .
By him be projected, or have him as your projection.

THE OPPOSITE OF INCARNATE

Every gnostic knows his need
To get out of blind flesh into knowing pneuma.
Spirit longs for spirit, to be freed,
While flesh feeds on flesh like a caged puma.

But the gnostic stumbles on the transformation
Of spirit into flesh as the way of escape,

Contingency, Poems 1989-2001

Rages against the demiurge of matter,
Denies any significance ever took shape.

That's not my struggle. I believe
God took up flesh, was made holy man.
I find it hardest to heartily affirm
I, so much flesh, also can.

PAPER SIGNIFICANCE

I set pen to paper -- hypocrite.
So you will know me as I write
That men are committed to paper
For their monuments now. Quite
Certain you are not significant,
Do not matter worth a damn,
Unless by means of paper
You prove, "I am";

And this is false, the enterprise
Shall surely in each case fail.
A grave and oblivious lie
At the end of each paper trail.
If we go on pursuing greatness
Of mind or soul or heart
In number of pages and volumes,
The whole will be a small part.

Dead men do not speak
Through lines printed over... and over.
They speak through the volumes
Of their lives, thin tracts, nothing more.
If a poem or essay or novel speaks
More than a grunt or sigh,

James Howard Trott

It is because a life saw truth
And said so. That's why
Myriad books now say so little.

As small children only parrot
What they hear a father or mother say,
Most write nothing of merit.

Merely howl or pant or slur
Empty sounds of animal night,
Ink run in inane blur.

I, too, write beyond myself,
Wish to conclude unbegun,
And with these words I do repent.
Write me a life, Dear Son.

BUSHWHACKING

In the thorn-thick busy bramble
Wilderness of woods
Your mind is hooked,
Your heart scratched,
By the general direction :
Where you want to go,
But can't -- not in a straight line.
You have to learn the little detours
Around the green briar,
And remember again --
Before the blackberry --
Where you were going.

Contingency, Poems 1989-2001

ELIEZER FISHING IN SAMARIA

A traveler waits beside a well -- so thirsty all.
He comes upon a mission knowing well his call --
Oh, did that we, in all things free.
Though what will come of it he wonders;
Somethings yet unclear he ponders --
Which fish she.

A woman goes outside the city -- as lovers do.
She comes to draw the moment's water, gone like dew --
So like our air, pure substance there.
Without the least of expectations
Someone sits, servant to nations,
Holds the long line's care.

From the fishing eagle's spiral -- how high he's got --
A white speck at the well returns, met by a dot --
We seem such motes, each aimless floats.
But back the speck, at the well lingers --
Some small matters are harbingers
Of eyrie notes.

Something precious he gives her -- memory made fast.
The brief sips she drew and gave him, her last.
(Our best compels no drop in hell)
Briefly back to her walled place,
She's bound already from her small race,
Pulled from the well.

BREAKING WEATHER

In these mountains
The storms and blue sky

James Howard Trott

Break suddenly on you --
As they do in life.

On the prairie
You can see them coming
Far away --
As in Christ's Kingdom.

USE US - THREE INTERPRETATIONS

Use us until we're strong enough
To use ourselves for higher purposes.

Use us until we have the strength
To throw you off and all using.

Use us until you use us up.

Of what use am I?

A BILLION DOLLAR ATTITUDE
(from a suggestion by Mike Moore and Brian Wood)

If that famous rich uncle
Known to myth-poor scholars
Died and left to me his
Hundred billion dollars,
I wouldn't know what to do
Anymore than most of you.

Contingency, Poems 1989-2001

I would try to receive it
Without acting too rude --
But, essentially, I lack
A billion dollar attitude!

EXPLICIT

She gives herself.
He is received.
She takes him in.
He gives her life.
What mystery
Do they subsume:
This perfect bride,
This spotless groom?

AZALEA WEATHER INDICATORS

The gnostic leaves of the azaleas
Outside our kitchen window
Curl ever more tightly
When temperatures drop.
When it's warm or merely chilly,
They hold the snow in flat handfuls,
Or welcome drops splashing
On their outstretched finger-palms,

On coldest days, a spinster,
Each holds her hands before her,
Leaves stiff and round, thin fingers.

Yet soon they will open
To hold purple bouquets,
Like warm brides in the blooming.

BALANCED ACCOUNT
(with V. A. Trott)

Dollars and cents
Daughters and sons,
If you've more of the others
You've less of the ones.

PREDATOR

Preying on all members of the ecosystem,
Is that one predator, the ecologist who lists 'em.

AS EACH LOVES

As each man loves his body
So you ought to love your wives.
Submit ye to each other,
Submit to your husbands your lives.

Contingency, Poems 1989-2001

As each man loves his wife,
So our Savior loves his Bride.
As each honors her husband,
So the church doth love her Christ.

As our Savior gave his body
For the church, so love your spouse:
As love is exchanged in heaven,
Let it be in thine own house.

THE WASTING OF OUR POWERS

The wasting of our powers consumes our hours,
Devours our days, incinerates our dust.
Our words tumble, are but the rumble
Of crumbling towers, counting cost in trust
Misplaced and dreams disgraced; traced in ink that fades,
While suns set; the proudest grow humble;
Memories forget and wander in parodies of charades;
Deaths laid hollow wastes where the worm worry cowers.

What powers had we? What hours sad we
Dropped through fingers, now that none lingers
To remind us of the loss. Tossed as spume and spray,
Every second, each day, each eon spent.
And all that we were lent, indeed every cent --
Whether million or ten -- shall be counted again.

James Howard Trott

ALIEN SHORES

I have traveled the long leagues into my neighbor's home.
I have watched the skies unfold under its wide dome.
I have heard forests whisper and seas crash
At his gate, and through his grate
Watched volcanoes pour out ash.

His is a distant clime, a decidedly foreign shore,
His sunrise and sunset resemble mine no more
Than his flora's flower, his fauna's sound
Bear a name, smell or skirr the same
As those within my bound.

I have converse with my neighbor. How can this be
Between two such alien ones as I and he?
It seems we both through memories dim
Recall a common sod,
A common stream, a common sun,
And dare I say . . .   God?

PUT IT OUT OF ITS MISERY

It took no philosophical education or logical regimen to sharpen up
My wits enough to hear a hollow ring (though I was a young pup)
In that expression applied to an unwanted pet, a litter of
Undesirable four-legged infants. I knew the misery out of
Which they were being put was not their own - nor misery no doubt,
Just inconvenience. How now that it's babies we put out?

Contingency, Poems 1989-2001

ABANDONED

The bow-legged hermit
Of a bared-bone shed.

The sway-backed beast
Of a faded barn.

A silent howl, empty door
Between staring windows.

Sunset-beacon pierced-side
Of a crucified cabin.

RABBIT TRAILS

Through the woods, through the grass
Run trails where rodents pass,
Roads for rabbits, mice and voles,
Familiar footpaths from nests and holes.

Through the hours of days of weeks
Of years a lifetime runs and seeks
Always the familiar forth and back
From door to grave, the trodden track.

But mice and hares are driven aside
Into briars and tall grass -- hide
Or search or pursue desire;
To escape the hawk, or hound or fire.

Men, too; minds, too, over protest
Are driven from ways they know best
Into the vast unknown, unknowing,
To a dim-trailed faith, narrow but growing.

James Howard Trott

BRIBES AND THREATS

These offered me what I could use,
What, indeed, I felt I needed
If only I would this ignore,
If only that more heeded.

Those told me I'd regret my choice,
Could well experience pain
Unless I did as they advised,
And was otherwise restrained.

Although I thought them different,
When they differed in their claims,
They traded roles so easily
I learned they were the same.

Truth stands apart from bribes and threats,
Needs tools nor long rehearsing.
From the same mouths in another sense
Will come both blessing and cursing.

YOUR TEARS ARE BLURRING MY VISION

Pardon me. . . I don't mean. . .
It's just there's so much to be seen. . .
No doubt it comes as a surprise
But your tears are starting to blur my eyes.

Don't let me interfere, impose. . .
You should just act naturally I suppose. . .
It's a matter of choice, it's your decision,
But your tears seem to be blurring my vision.

Contingency, Poems 1989-2001

I can't see all the lovely things,
I want to see, that my heart sings.
I'm stuck here in this gray wet fog
With your tears in my eyes --
Whose speck. . . whose log?

If sufficient to the day is the evil thereof,
Then I've troubles enough -- don't say love
Means crying other tears, feeling other pain --
We're all on our own -- don't start again!

But my heart won't let my eyes be silent,
And my soul refuses to be an island,
In spite of myself I'm caught in a flood
Flowed from one who shed my blood.

Pardon me . . .   I don't mean . . .
It's just that there's so much to be seen . . .
No doubt it comes as a surprise
But your tears continue to blur my eyes.

RIGHT INDEX

I've finally done it -- what I've long prided myself
In avoiding through superior foresight and care--
Run my finger through the table saw in relatively
Minor accident, taken in comparison to others
I've heard of and of which I've seen the scars.

They say the centre in the brain for speech is, too,
The nexus of prestidigitation, thus the natural
Transfer of talk to finger language among various
Colorful peoples -- native Americans, Italians,
Jewish shopkeepers, the unhearing, and typists.

James Howard Trott

And most central, not only to communication, but also
In doing, this right index amidst bandages is sorely missed,
And piously interceded for in hopes it will recover,
Rather than grow infected and -- worst case -- be lost,
Rather like the boy in the saw-poem by Frost.

The wounding of this finger throws all in a cocked hat:
I feel like a disciple on Friday or the Shabbat.
My world turned about this small jointed axis,
And now I am all unfit in theory and praxis,
Longing for the bandages to be rolled aside.

My left hand and the remaining three try their best,
To fill the gap, but their efforts are not blessed.
The wounded right, index for others' direction,
Embalmed in its bandage points straight ahead,
As the rest of me prays fervently for resurrection.

WHERE IS GOD WHEN IT HURTS?

Where is God when it hurts?
Is He on the moon?
Is He at the office
Promising to come home soon?

Is He on vacation?
Or perhaps addressing the nation?
Is he busy fretting
Over someone else's wine
At someone else's wedding?

Or is he largely sympathetic,
But quite unable
To empathize, answering our moans
Like Scarlet O'Hare's Clark Gable ?

Contingency, Poems 1989-2001

Where is God when it hurts?
Where is anyone
While he's chastising
His daughter or his son?

FAITH'S ANTONYMS

Set not faith against works, Oh Luther's quirks,
We respect them, we understand, but they must be banned
From our perspective which willy-nilly, grows
Making yesterday's opposition silly.

Faith, says Lewis (C.S.), is not the antithesis
Of knowledge, no, though moderns would have it so,
Rather of emotion, the urge, not the notion.

Or as a brother once said, sat by hospital bed,
The opposite of faith is not reason (he cited Abram's season
Of wandering after God's surety) rather it's security.

Faith is opposed to seeing, sometimes to knowing or being.
Though faith be opposed by many, it isn't opposed to any.
Faith is invisible as a germ to the eye,
And is best defined by its cotermini.

THE WELDER'S TORCH

The welder's torch
Gives off

James Howard Trott

A blinding light
Whether it cuts or connects
Whether it hurts or heals.
It can only be seen directly
Through dark filters and lenses --
So dark that
When one puts them on
All else becomes
Dim and obscure --
All but the torch of the welder.

A SAW ONLY CUTS WHEN IT MOVES

A butterknife, a sword, even a laser move to cut.
All the plans, the talk, the theological diagrams on earth
Slice no bread, unless the church is moving,
On blessed sawtooth feet, rightly dividing the truth.

WALKING TOWARD MY FATHER WALKING AWAY FROM ME.

I walked toward my father who walked away from me.
It was inevitable he should,
I'm not the one he wanted,
Couldn't be.

I walked toward my father who walked away from me,
And knew, he, too,
Looked for a father's
Company.

I walked toward my father who walked away from me --
Then turned, aggrieved but free
To speak to you of us,
Fathers three.

SIN BOUND

Sin bound, bound to sin,
Stained in utero, where we begin
At heart's first bound, strained, intent
On a bounder's course, a lifetime spent
In boundless capacity to deprave,
Then bundled at last into the grave.

Sin bound, bound to out,
Buried how deep, hid beyond doubt,
Beneath propriety or discipline
Bursting forth manifold, mighty sin
Demanding its right of place
In every heart, on every face.

Sin bound, banded in bond
To carry the battle where none had gone,
To be bound by sin to break sin's bindings
To reverse the court by fulfilling its findings,
God, the Father, the Son and the Ghost
Bound sin to a cross-barred and bloody post.

James Howard Trott

UNFINISHED BUSINESS

A garage full of ancient furniture,
A basement of household repairs,
A dusty attic of incomplete thoughts
At the top of a dusty stairs ;

A drawer full of estimates,
List of awaiting-replies,
A pile of unfinished poems,
Too over- or too under-sized --

Beside the names long-unspoken,
And the lives languished and lorning,
And the hope-not-quite-expectation
We'll get to it all in the morning.

EVERY MAN'S HOUR

Every man has a time and a place,
A row to hoe, a calling, a race.
Every man has a job to do:
Truth to love, loves to which to be true.

TOUCH AND GO
"It still seems kind of touch and go"

When we first touched hands
It was free and easy in courtesy and jest.
Immediately we touched minds and
The public appendages of heart;

Contingency, Poems 1989-2001

Then made more formal meeting,
And soberly touched intellects,
With a final first spiritual intimacy.

Always between the gestures,
As always thereafter, between the meetings,
We retreated,
Drew back in a step or dance,
The prance not of coquetry, at least not just,
The back and forth of tremor,
And of trust.

When we first touched lips, it was brief,
We both knew we could easily come
To that sorrow which is lingering too long --
A kind of departure.
Our touching and our going
Must have been as they were --
Neither eclipsing the other, neither
The single motive of our souls.

But when we wed, our thought it might
Be forever touching and hardly ever going
Gradually sank subsumed in surprise
At the need of both, a spurt of growth
In departing and drawing close;
Gnosis of merger and divergence the theme,
No Hollywood dream, but still touching and going.

And now, yet, we flounder at failure
To formulate, may get, but often miss
The equation of a kiss
Or the right blessing at the right moment,
Addressing our reflected selves. Such
Indirection harries and hinders
Both going and mutual knowing
In many a touch.

James Howard Trott

And where we have gotten very good
At certain kinds of going, at cluing in
To cues and curtains;
Where we are masters of certain touches,
The worlds best lovers,
Little covers our naked in-betweens,
The shabby means.

It is still touch and go with us --
Still a dance, still a dizzying
Lesson and so much
Like going with God; like feeling God's touch.

STARING AT THE SUN

You can do it. The thing can be done
Your eyes will work for a while if you
Stare at the sun.

Just as reason and your analytical powers
Can be directed at God and linger there
Some hours.

But the burnout and blindness
Will not be superstitions:
Nor awe and mental fatigue
Coincidental conditions.

Eyes are too frail in constitution
To comprehend solar facts:
Minds, though glimpsing God's grandeur,
Can seldom follow his acts.

Contingency, Poems 1989-2001

> Only people out of their senses
> Dare stare when the sun is bright,
> But every creature on earth walks
> And sees all else in its light.

TOBACCO SMOKE AND COFFEE

The incense that stole through that cloister
Where I was novitiate
Came in two dominant bouquets --
The evening pipe of my father
And the morning coffee of my mother's kitchen.
Neither essence attracted me to the concrete.
They were indeed essences to mind and memory,
Remain distinct from substantial tobacco and coffee.

How strange that the child can most enjoy
What he could not bear to imbibe;
Or is it that the essence of things is always apprehended
At our simpler moments by our subtler senses.

TETHER BALL

> Whirls the sphere on a tautened chord
>   tethered to its unmoved ends;
> Closes quickly in tightening arcs;
>   tangled more surely, to its tether tends.

James Howard Trott

Two ends there are, two paths of gyre,
    twy spirals spun and spanked in heat
By fierce opponents with one desire:
    the ball's capture, the other's defeat.

At those moments when all seems hopeless :
    the globe speeding close in tilting track,
One turns his hand to his own defeat
        -- one moment --
    then drives the ball hurtling back.

TIME TO BE GLORIFIED

    The low light
    Sliding under the storm
    Shot the shoddy tops of trees
    With dazzling dusk,
    Belying their dying --
    Red and transparent glory.

THE THINKER

    Jesus, my head is sunken down.
    Lift it up to see thy crown,
    To see thee on thy sovereign throne --
    Instead of brooding on my own.

Contingency, Poems 1989-2001

THERE IS A BURGLAR IN MY HOUSE

There is a burglar in my house, but if I close my eyes . . .
I need not see his shadow loom
Or watch him slide into my room,
While huddled blind upon my bed, avoiding all surmise.

Though foreign footsteps dust my floor, by covering my ears
. . . I needn't know that they encroach
Upon my world; that their approach
Portends unheard of fatal facts that might fulfill my fears.

A presence ponders in my room, but if I do not feel . . .
A fancy I may entertain
That it's a phantom of my brain,
Which touches nothing tangible, nor anything can steal.

A hand clamps upon my mouth, but if I do not stir . . .
Possibly it will go away,
And nothing do and nothing say,
Ignoring me as I do it, and reciproc'ly unsure.

There is a burglar in my house -- my <u>own</u> little place . . .
His presence here despite my walls,
In rustlings and foot-falls
Almost opens awful thoughts -- of meeting face to face.

FRUITING DUE TO TRAUMA

The wild buckwheat in my hedges is so perverse
It can produce its "nuts" after I've torn its roots,
From the ground, done my worst, so that when I yank
Its shriveled stem, the fruits roll down among
The ivy vines, too rank to permit me to find all,
Until next spring they've sprung.

James Howard Trott

In a hot summer like we just had the blackberries
Do poorly, but nevertheless do their best to be,
And the hardest hit carries its sacrifices to extreme,
Sending all the sap of its tiny tree to its drupes,
Which burgeon from that thin stream, ripen sweet
As the dead plant stoops.

And desert flowers, I am told, take bold advantage
Of the brief showers that dampen the sand.
Then barely manage to blossom, fruit and seed before
They too fade at the sun's demand and wither to stalks
Nothing more, except for the tiny germs they've left,
Treasure under sand-grain locks.

The mystery mobile plant, plasmodium or slime mold
Moves across the forest floor when times are flush
A bit like jello, boldly crawling its slow path
Over log, beneath bush, until conditions become cold or dry.
Then sensing a fallen Nature's wrath, it becomes
A fruiting form, prepared to die.

Some mushrooms, and some lowly herbs flourish and flower
Best along paths where feet and wheels beat hard the ground
Pressed with death hour after hour. Some trees release cones
Only when fire surrounds them in pyric panorama
Likewise flora of the human zone -- how many fruitings
Are due to trauma.

SUDDEN FROST

The magnolia that boomed beauty
Basking in the adulation of spring
Is suddenly brown and wilted --
Every blossom hanging dead like
Autumn roses or rags of a prom dress.

Contingency, Poems 1989-2001

The short frost brought to an end
Its show of life and purpose --
But the small plum blossoms remain;
Smile small but alive
Against their bleak black bark.

THE THIRD STORM
(For Nancy Long)

Facing the first storm, I mustered strength,
Measured the storm line, breadth and length,
And made ready to meet it with my resources,
My resolve, my courage: my own inner forces --
And I survived.

Facing the second storm, I quailed with a taste
A doubt, remembering what I'd faced
Of suffering, of anguish, of lingering pain
Beyond my calculations -- Could I weather again?
But seeing there was no escape, no place of flight or shelter,
I entered that one, too, like ore into a smelter --
And I survived.

When the third storm arose after years of calm,
I knew I could not make it -- not just a qualm,
But a certainty that knowing what I knew about desolation
My heart and mind would crumble, straw in conflagration.
And I cried out -- for a miracle, power beyond me --
Which miraculously reached out and strangely found me.
Now I stand in the storm and wonder at this dark-hid grace,
Waiting and hoping beyond the storm to see a face --
Much more than surviving.

James Howard Trott

STRIPPED BODY ON A CROSS

They stripped him naked before nailing him to the cross,
A small loss, ones clothing, ones dignity, ones esteem
It would seem to us, who pain and death fear most,
And boast of our physiques, honoring the nude,
Calling any a prude who demurs or complains,
With post-Edenic strains of hiding and shame,
For we claim the prior prerogatives of pride and fruit.

His family and friends, however, especially the women,
Bravely incriminating themselves by final association,
Found that station agonical and extreme not only
In the lonely innocent at whose death they stood vigilant,
But the peculiar circumstant that they could not look,
As that old book of crotchety Isaiah predicted of Messiah,
A pariah beyond the beholding of his own.

His nakedness was more for them than embarrassment,
It rent the curtain of their kindred bonds and rites,
Made his journey into night solitary beyond seeing,
Nearly beyond human being, and forced their vision
To the admission that if hope or solace was to be found,
It was bound up in his unseen purposes; that parts
Would be naked until, the body gone, faith clothed hearts.

TIME TO KILL

David on the rooftop had time to kill,
Time the murderer sloped along his sight,
By way of the washroom on Uriah's roof,
A woman's body, and a whoop-it-up night.

Contingency, Poems 1989-2001

Time to kill hangs on our hands:
Time to myself, to rest, time stands
Still; then rushes on; clock hands spin:
Time-to-go-out soon time-to-come-in.

Time is the miser's irretrievable craving,
The substance sought by every and all,
But beyond all and anyone's saving.
Time is the watchman that shines his torch
Into every window, every bedroom and porch
And reveals what's happened there,
Who cowers behind the facade.
Time is the foreman in the factory of God.

But we fool ourselves once in a while,
Now and then, occasionally
And think time ours to use, to spend
Or patiently -- to kill.

Then it is that like David's frantic hands
Ours reach for other lives to spend
To satisfy our demands:
A husband's, a wife's, perhaps a child's unborn.
Time to kill become killing time
Becomes a long time to mourn.

THE SPLINTER
(For Loren)

This splinter you and I picked up somewhere
Doesn't act as splinters should --
Although it's often infected,
That doesn't do much good,
For instead of slipping out then,
It just stabs further in,

Until it feels like that three letter word
In the seat of our hearts (S _ _!)
The question where did we pick it up
Plagues us from time to time,
An issue to mumble and fume about,
To occupy us -- like rhyme.
We don't see why others so blithely
Trip along through love and life
Without our sort of sharp splinter.
(Ouch! That hurt like a knife!)
When we most despair in discomfort,
And are nearly convinced it's fatal
Our physician reminds us he dealt with
Splinters, too – from cross, crown, and cradle.

COMMUNION IMAGES

The torn and tortured crumb for me,
The royal purple healing sweet,
The eye winking in the cup,
The horror of this kind of meat.
The sword cutting on the tongue,
Overmastering it's deadly thrusts,
The clumsy men's hands and feet
Dusty treasured things to trust.
The empty stains upon the table,
Speaking better things than Abel.

Contingency, Poems 1989-2001

ONE OF THE WORLD'S BEST LOVERS

The world's best lover, he said, and lovely she
Replied in kind with jot of jest, not <u>one</u> of the best.
Strange how one connoting so much, at just a tittle
Turns into something other, grown less and little :
Where quantity so contrary to excellence and the lack
Of experience surest sign of knowledge and the knack.

The world says no -- good technique and earned esteem
Are acquired in love as in trade, sports or cuisine:
Opponents encountered, the more menus we prepare,
The subtler our skills, the more delectable our fare.

Our lovers, Love, are so very few -- indeed are but one.
More would be so many fewer, less love, less fun.

The world might be more faithful if only the world knew:
One of the world's best lovers must be but one of two.

OBITUARY FOR FRANCIS WHITTINGTON

Francis Whittington dead a week today
Had season tickets, saw the Phillies play,
She and her sister watched losses and winnings
Until she entered the final innings.

Three years ago they cut off one of her legs,
And she ended up in the nursing home.
(My children were awed to meet someone
With only one leg) yet always her tone
Was humorous, hearty, cheerful, straight,
Like an umpire calling you out at the plate.

James Howard Trott

My children's hearts went out to her,
We looked for her to help us sing
Amazing Grace and Old Rugged Cross
And I Come to the Garden . She'd a ring
To her voice that would lift and meld
Like a leading fan when the crowd yelled.

I had never met anyone she called kin,
But at the funeral there were seven,
A brother, an in-law, nephews and niece,
Who had barely heard of her decease.

The sister had died but a month before,
Who had lived with Francis for many a day.
They two were partners in sports and crime --
Famous Phillies fans in their time.

A couple from her church and the new pastor there
Completed the numbers at her service and burial --
Not quite the crowd you'd see at a game,
But to Francis I'm sure it was immaterial.

Her other leg killed her -- gangrene --
On which she stole home almost unseen,
Where God's Son put her ahead by one,
And angels cheered for Whittington.

THE RIGHT WAY TO RESPOND TO A GIFT
(after Jed's 8th birthday)

The gift-gone boy so overflows with delight,
His body leaps further than his mind's insight.
The joy of his heart rebounds such a distance,
That his arms and legs drive up and down like pistons.

Contingency, Poems 1989-2001

LIGHT OF A CERTAIN KIND
(On a Fragment of Labradorite)

Universal light is a metaphor for truth, for its revealing,
But there is more to revelation than a spotlight on a stage,
Showing up stark fact by simply appealing to common vision,
Common experience, common understanding (common to every
 age),
Since seers, and feelers and knowers are more complex than that
Just as truth is, and its showing, nor is light so pat.

There are many kinds of light, many facets, filtrates, and forms
According to spectroanalysis and photography. Light is a being
With variations always more than our norms quite admit to;
And objects, too, may seem variously peculiar to our seeing
When shown in a certain light of a certain angle or hue,
Forcing us to keep alert toward seeing something new.

Thus a gray stone found in bed of mountain stream may surprise
One as one did me when sudden blue beams blew ablaze
And as quickly, when I moved, ceased for my eyes, 'til moved
 back.
Other minerals show brilliant only beneath ultraviolet rays;
And clouds variously : for white - noondays; for crimson -
 sunsets.
What glows in the dark shows best when night's as dark as it
 gets.

LEAST LEADING

If you want sober leaders, make them read, "Whatsoever you do
Unto the least of these my brethren, you do so unto me."

The Lord leads, and leans on us to minister to the least:
Widow, orphan, stranger, alien, lame, deaf, and blind –
And, everywhere and always, children-kind.

But, too, he sets these up as leaders in a kingdom, church,
Always headed by incompetents of exemplary weakness.

Thus on Christmas morning, my six children,
(Some now adults) have always assigned holy orders,
Heading the procession to the place of gifts,
To the youngest: leave it always to the least to lead.

"The last shall be first, and the first shall be last."
Becomes more than dire prophecy -- a divine courtesy.

THE TRULY SELF-RIGHTEOUS

The truly self-righteous keep close to sinners,
Worship with publicans, an eye on the whore.
The truly self-righteous value the contrast,
Accumulate evidence in a rainy-day store.
The truly self-righteous are regular, helpful,
Reach out to the needy (wearing thick gloves).
The truly self-righteous know all about Jesus --
Except that he lives, and except that he loves.

IN MEMORY OF ETHEL VILE

Some Sundays she offered little but sighs,
Only asking prayer for her sick grandson.
Sometimes she offered a joke and a smile,
That kindly told, this patiently done,
But more than she offered we knew we'd lost
When they told us this week Ethel died.

Vile is death counting earthly cost :
Not noble to any who yet must abide.
She, president of the resident's board,
A big wheel on two, confined to the chair,
Had family that flourished in the hauling trade.
Did the name contribute to getting them there,
A living disposing of garbage made ?
She suffered many who found it funny,
This honest way they made their money.
But "vile" comes from "villain, which meant
But a common man, often a servant sent
About the business of one more exalted,
Like the highest Servant, who cannot be faulted.
And Ethel means "noble" in Old English tongue;
Noble we knew her -- our little while.
She reminds us God transforms whomever he hauls
Once Vile, now it's always on Ethel he calls .

UNDERWHELMED

Many who grew up with the mountains looming there,
Blue, green, white, gray, found they rarely noticed
Their magnificence, just as those grown by the sea,
Turn to other sources of majesty for inspiration.

The woodsman sees little of the forest or the trees,
Nor is the plainsman impressed by these panoramas.
The Arab feels little reverence for deserts. Snow
Elicits small poetry from the native Eskimo.

So the terrain of my soul, the Himalayas and Gobis of sin
Underwhelm me who has dwelt so long therein.
And worse yet, Lord, get me out of every place,
Where I grow underwhelmed by the glory of your grace.

James Howard Trott

VISION FROM OUR HOUSE

A robin through an old window pane
Comes and goes and comes again --
Not behind trees or tufts of grass,
But behind imperfections of our glass.

A WARM FRONT

Raindrops stamp the sheer planes of my walled sufficiency.
Their echoes invade with cosmic news,
The bulk mail of the universe.

GERRY'S DEPARTURE

Gerry came humbly into our lives and living--
She smiled and spoke softly, and gently began giving
To friend after friend, the lively and the lonely,
Until her heart failed -- her heart, the organ, only . . .

She encouraged us so servantly, we scarcely knew she did;
Sounded no alms-trumpet : no pro quo for her quid.
She lived just out of sight, obscure amidst charity,
Until she slipped from us, leaving a kind of clarity.

In her hospital room she suffered another heart attack,
From which the doctor felt he could not bring her back,
But at her daughter's own heart's cry, "Mommy, don't go yet!"
Gerry her course delayed, her other heart's habit.

Contingency, Poems 1989-2001

She remained another few weeks, here for the holiday,
Gave last hugs and kisses, gave everyone their say.
Then, when she had served us all with all her life and breath,
Deferring no longer, she bowed briefly to death.

Merciful like our Christ, with similar self-less lenience,
Gerry arranged her life for us
      . . . and her death at our convenience.

HIGHER GLYPHICS

The mysterious inkspot
On Wittenburg's stony wall
Testifies the devil frightens
Men, great and small.
The finer print written there
In trickle and in splatter,
He flees who'e'er fights back in faith, --
Your missiles matter.

DETRITUS AND TREASURES

The piece of pottery,
The antique chair,
Each memorial of ancestral splendor
May be but detritus of death,
Nostalgiac pretender.

James Howard Trott

But priceless things on bright display,
Passed beyond dust of tombs --
Not on our shelves,
Or museum vaults --
Are displayed in many rooms.

DESPERATE ROSE

Love is a word, is a feeling, a thing, is someone
Who, which, disappears far more readily than the reverse,
Like the bloom in everybody's grandmother's yard;
Like the mysterious speck on the surface of my eye
Seen at times when I lie on my back all unfocused,
Love can seldom be directly regarded for long, but fades away
Until we consent to let him, let it creep along the periphery --
The wallflower at every wedding or funeral.
But love does not hide for lack of passion.
Usually poorly, but in this thing accurately,
Love is portrayed by its imitators -- intent, intense, desperate
-- Love blossoms on a wall, a frame, or a tree
Desperately giving itself to me.

WE DOUBT

I don't expect what's lost to be found.
She doubts we'll fix what's broken.
We both lose hope that right will reign,
That truth will ever be spoken.

Contingency, Poems 1989-2001

Some might see wisdom in our doubts
At this hour of the thief,
But we still fight what lies in our hearts,
And call it unbelief.

WHAT THE SNOW DID

The snow fleshed the bones of the tree,
Keeping me home from work,
Crumbling though that clothing be,
It fell as blessed flesh to me.

The snow clothed the naked limbs,
Called a quarantine against the curse
Robed a while in brighter trim,
Than leaves ever : a triumph hymn.

The tree was enlarged with glory snow
And I chafed a bit to be set free,
Though bits of light tore away and blew,
Wind made of the tree a story I know.

The snow hugged the tree out of sight,
Forced on me my insignificance,
Clock-muffling day swallowed night
And bark-black darkness bowed under light.

DELIVER ME INTO THE DEEP

Not " sinking deep in sin"
   But wading up to my knees.

James Howard Trott

Not "far from the peaceful shore "
    But in shallow, easy seas.
Tangled in gently gathering weeds,
    Caressing my limbs as they ride
Together with flotsam and jetsam,
    The weft of the daily tide.

Lost as much in disgruntlement
    As depraved or deprived or asleep . . .
Come, Lord. Again deliver me
    -- Into the Deep
(Where, indeed I needed you,
    Needed you or drowned.)
Deliver me into the deep,
    Oh, Lord, where You are found.

LOCKSMITH : KEYS MADE

As we turn against the wards of life,
The brass guardians of what lies beyond,
We wonder why so much is locked,
So few ways easy to enter upon.

We must grate against combinations,
Obstacles arranged to try our true,
And only when our ground edge fits,
Do doors click open and let us through.

Yet others pass through where we bind,
Their own wards made to fit the lock,
Their strengths and weaknesses of peculiar grind
Among the myriad of the Locksmith's stock.

Contingency, Poems 1989-2001

THE COMPANION
(For Two Sisters At the Nursing Home)

I see a woman walk hand in hand
With an crippled image of herself:
Plain and normal with wracked awry,
Linked in each other's double grip.

Mind in mind I see the world,
Images skewed intertwined with true:
Memories, imaginations clasping others
Too wrong to be real, brothers.

The defect in strand, or strain of birth
That warped the figure planned by God
Was planned by God; allowed and planned,
To lead her sister by the hand.

WHY WE IGNORE THE DYING

Because they were so successful
Or because they failed.
Because beside their groaning
Our causes of groaning paled.

Because they tell old stories
Or because they hardly hear us.
Because they seem to want us.
Because they seem to fear us.

Because they are so sloppy,
Or because they stay so spruce.
Because she is a freight train
Or because he's a caboose.

James Howard Trott

Because they were so incredible
Or because they were credible barely
Or because to continue to love them,
One must face death squarely.

CLEAN HANDS

Mucking about as I have been
Clean hands sound good,
To be free of sin's stink,
Sin's stain, sins stick
Is indeed attractive, so what's the trick?

A blood-bath! Say, that's a bit kinky --
Like washing in paint
Because you're inky... no.
You say its the only way?
Bring on this gore that cleans as you say.

Ah! Clean -- good gracious -- as a whistle!
Pure and soft
Like down on a thistle. I'll pass the word,
It's too good to be true.
Spotless is great -- can I pay you?

No, well thanks, I'm bound up-hill!
What's that you say?
There's work here still? A job
Something like the one you did me?
These clean hands crucified! You're kidding me!

Made clean to prevent infection!
I thought the purpose

Was to pass inspection! Ready?
For nails! I don't easily heal!
Aha, so that's the catch in this deal.

BLACK WALNUTS

Who quickest offends may be
Found best friend ;
The easy-pleasing in every season
Most prone to treason.
The best Quaker
Will not celebrate ;
Best Catholic --
To Rome and Mary true
(or celibate) ;
Best Baptist, won't drink,
Except in the font
(Only after he believes) ;
The truest Pentecostal grieves
At who receives
Not a second, Spirit baptism.
These brethren are like
Those other, best of nuts :
With sweetest meat --
And hardest shell --
Sweet as heaven,
And hard as hell.

James Howard Trott

BETWEEN

The first division and the last;
An old creation and deathless new;
Earthly paradise and heavenly home;
All things false and all things true.

Everlasting fire and the altar coal;
The roaring beast and Judah's lion;
The serpent's first words and his last;
Mount Gerazim and the greater Zion.

The flood of water and the flood of blood;
Brief Babel and perfect Pentecost;
Leaves and skins and shining robes;
Much good found and all bad lost.

Mount Sinai and the Mount of Olives;
The Last Supper and the first;
A furtive feast and a wedding toast;
A killing hunger and a living thirst.

The Red and the Crystal Seas;
Abel's blood, the stream from the throne;
Jonah's Whale and an empty grave;
Israel's Jordan and my own.

WITHOUT PRACTICE

Among the tests doctors endure, it cannot be the least
That long after medical school exams and such have certainly ceased,
He or she must listen to second rate jokes cracked as
The chuckling patient enquires again about medical "practice?"

Contingency, Poems 1989-2001

Runners and players and singers and actresses
All must work hard at their various practices.
The speaker and preacher, minister or priest,
All need some practice, at first at least.

But doctors practice like apprentices in trades,
By performing their profession (and not for grades).
They don't take "trial runs"; furthermore the fact is,
That's also true of faith that is practiced.

I AM THE PROPRIETOR OF THE BASEBALL BOOTH

    I am the proprietor of the baseball booth,
    Advertising my potential down the broad midway.
    Step right up, win your gal a kewpie doll.
    Putting up targets, bright and insubstantial.

    I don't want anyone to get a hit, to win a prize,
    To slip inside my carefully devised scheme,
    Where I am in control, and I take your money,
    And you takes your chances (poor they seem).

    My targets are weighted and heavily fringed,
    The real me, the hurts, the longings are well-hidden.
    Pay your money, three throws for a dollar.
    No man, no woman, not even God can hit my targets.

    I am the proprietor of the baseball booth.
    Pay and throw, as I direct you --
    At targets I have carefully prepared and arrange --
    No! You fool! Don't throw at me!

James Howard Trott

BEING HUGGED BEHIND MY BACK

My sweet pea, in her sixth year,
Heard me playing the piano here;
Stole up behind and wrapped a hug
Around my waist. Her small arms bare
Were all I could see of her love, embrace,
Though soon I'll hug her face to face.

As she loved me, no more than a back
And a poorly played tune, no lack
Of seeing her can diminish her squeezes
Nor future hugs, from her or Jesus.

YOU NEVER PICK TRASH IN YOUR OWN NEIGHBORHOOD

Of course in a small town like my native one,
A native son knew instinctively
That propinquity extended the breadth and length,
The strength of community eyes and ears and feeling
Sealing all discards as taboo,
At least until hauled away,
Which is to say, as afar as the town dump.
There one might gather objects spent
To full measure of one's heart's content.

But along this city street,
Being discreet extends only so far
As people know who you are,
Or know your car or truck,
So that any with pluck and inclination
May forestall incineration of objects thought redeemable,

Esteemable in imagination's eye,
'Why, with just a small repair. . .'
The chair, the bureau, the antique iron
Beckons us like the ancient siren.

Yet the mysterious taboo stands here as well.
It takes a will of steel or idiocy of a kind,
To openly never mind what the neighbors think
And recover a thrown-out sink, or stool, or shelves
They themselves put out.
It seems a challenge, offense,
An implication of folly,
(No matter how apparently good) like God
To gather trash in your own neighborhood.

ALPENGLOW

The glow that rises from the flower at dusk
Like the roses musk
Exceeds sense --

Like the fire that flares, the embers' gasp,
Beyond the grasp
Of time and tense --

So this light that looms out of snow and trees,
Stooping on the frieze
Of high eminence :

Alpenglow.

James Howard Trott

www.ingramcontent.com/pod-product-compliance
Lightning Source LLC
Chambersburg PA
CBHW070550050426
42450CB00011B/2795